AI with Azure: Buil Application

I0009910

First Edition

Preface

The advent of Artificial Intelligence (AI) has marked a new era in the technological landscape, reshaping industries, redefining human-machine interaction, and unlocking possibilities previously confined to the realm of science fiction. As organizations strive to stay competitive in an increasingly data-driven world, AI has become a pivotal component of digital transformation strategies. Microsoft Azure, with its robust suite of cloud-based services, stands at the forefront of this revolution, offering developers, data scientists, and IT professionals a powerful platform to build, deploy, and scale AI solutions.

This book, *AI with Azure: Build Smarter Applications*, is the 1st Edition in a series aimed at making the vast world of Azure AI accessible to everyone—from curious newcomers to aspiring machine learning engineers and enterprise architects. Whether you're looking to explore AI fundamentals, experiment with Azure Cognitive Services, or integrate intelligent features into your applications, this book provides a comprehensive roadmap for leveraging Azure's capabilities efficiently and ethically.

Spanning from foundational setup to advanced deployment strategies, this book is designed to be both practical and educational. Each chapter walks you through critical concepts, tools, and real-world examples, culminating in a holistic understanding of AI in the Azure ecosystem. Along the way, we'll delve into essential topics such as ethical AI practices, performance optimization, and hybrid cloud deployments with Azure Arc.

The structure of the book ensures that each concept builds upon the previous one. You'll start with the basics—understanding Azure's role in AI development and setting up your environment—before diving into hands-on applications like using Cognitive Services and Azure Machine Learning Studio. Later chapters explore integration with web and mobile apps, constructing secure and scalable data pipelines, and tackling the real-world challenges of deploying AI responsibly.

What sets this book apart is its focus on practical implementation. With curated code snippets, architectural tips, and sample projects, you'll gain the skills to move from theory to practice with confidence. The appendices include a glossary, additional resources, and frequently asked questions, making it a valuable reference for continued learning.

As AI technology continues to evolve, so too must our understanding and approach. This book is not just a guide—it's an invitation to become an active participant in the future of AI on Azure. Whether you're building your first intelligent chatbot or architecting a predictive analytics platform for global use, this book will help you unlock the full potential of AI in the cloud.

Welcome to your Azure AI journey.

Table of Contents

Chapter 1: Introduction to AI in the Azure Ecosystem

The Evolution of AI and Cloud Computing

The history of Artificial Intelligence (AI) is one marked by both exhilarating innovation and daunting challenges. From its early conception in the mid-20th century to the deep learning breakthroughs of the 2010s, AI has evolved from rule-based systems to self-learning algorithms capable of driving cars, interpreting human language, and diagnosing diseases. Parallel to this evolution has been the meteoric rise of cloud computing, which has fundamentally reshaped how data is stored, processed, and distributed.

In the past, AI development required vast computational resources that were often out of reach for all but the most well-funded research institutions. The cloud changed that. With scalable infrastructure, pay-as-you-go pricing models, and a suite of AI-ready services, cloud platforms like Microsoft Azure have democratized access to powerful computing tools. Today, even small startups can harness the same resources as tech giants to build, train, and deploy AI models at scale.

From Mainframes to the Cloud: A Timeline

- **1950s–1960s**: The birth of AI theory, with pioneers like Alan Turing and John McCarthy laying the groundwork.

- **1970s–1980s**: The first "AI winters" slow development due to lack of computational power and overpromising.

- **1990s**: The emergence of expert systems, rudimentary NLP, and early machine learning.

- **2000s**: Explosion of data and storage capacity opens doors for data-driven AI models.

- **2010s**: Cloud computing and GPU acceleration catalyze deep learning; cloud services begin offering ML capabilities.

- **2020s**: Hybrid AI, ethical AI, and edge computing take center stage, with Azure as a leading platform.

The convergence of AI and cloud computing has also given rise to a new development paradigm. Developers no longer need to understand the intricacies of tensor algebra or design neural network architectures from scratch to implement AI. Instead, they can rely on pre-built APIs, drag-and-drop interfaces, and integrated development environments offered by platforms like Azure.

AI as a Cloud-First Citizen

Microsoft Azure treats AI not as an add-on, but as a core component of its ecosystem. Key offerings such as Azure Machine Learning, Cognitive Services, and Azure Databricks allow for every phase of the AI lifecycle to be handled in the cloud. These tools support:

- Data   ingestion   and   preparation

- Model   training   and   evaluation

- Deployment   and   monitoring

- Governance   and   ethical   compliance

Moreover, Azure's commitment to open-source technologies and hybrid environments means you're never locked in. You can use popular frameworks like PyTorch, TensorFlow, and scikit-learn in conjunction with Azure services, while also deploying models to on-premises servers or edge devices using Azure Arc and IoT Edge.

The Shift from Hardware-Centric to Service-Oriented AI

In traditional AI workflows, the emphasis was heavily placed on managing hardware—choosing the right CPUs/GPUs, ensuring adequate RAM, configuring networking for distributed training. Azure abstracts these concerns, offering services such as:

```
# Creating a GPU-enabled Azure Machine Learning compute instance
az ml compute create --name gpu-cluster \
                --type AmlCompute \
                --min-instances 0 \
                --max-instances 4 \
                --size Standard_NC6
```

This shift allows developers to focus more on model architecture, feature engineering, and business logic rather than infrastructure overhead.

Empowering All Skill Levels

Perhaps one of the most transformative aspects of Azure's AI capabilities is accessibility. Beginners can explore pre-trained models and no-code solutions like Azure ML Designer, while advanced users can build custom pipelines with Python SDKs and REST APIs.

For example, a beginner might use the Face API to detect emotions in images with a simple HTTP call:

```
POST                                                    https://<your-
region>.api.cognitive.microsoft.com/face/v1.0/detect
```

```
Headers:
  Content-Type: application/json
  Ocp-Apim-Subscription-Key: YOUR_KEY

Body:
{
  "url": "https://example.com/photo.jpg"
}
```

Meanwhile, a data scientist could run hyperparameter tuning with the AzureML SDK:

```
from  azureml.train.hyperdrive  import  RandomParameterSampling,
HyperDriveConfig
from azureml.train.estimator import Estimator

param_sampling = RandomParameterSampling({
    "learning_rate": uniform(0.001, 0.1),
    "batch_size": choice(16, 32, 64)
})

hd_config = HyperDriveConfig(estimator=Estimator(...),
                             hyperparameter_sampling=param_sampling,
                             max_total_runs=20,
                             max_concurrent_runs=4)
```

Democratization of AI

In summary, the evolution of AI has been significantly accelerated by the rise of cloud computing. Azure exemplifies this by offering a full-stack approach to AI development—from data ingestion and processing to model deployment and monitoring. This democratization means that anyone with an internet connection and a curiosity for AI can begin building intelligent applications.

Azure's AI ecosystem is robust, modular, and scalable. Whether you're building a simple chatbot or architecting a multilingual voice assistant for global deployment, Azure provides the tools, infrastructure, and flexibility needed to bring your vision to life.

In the following sections, we'll dive deeper into why Azure is a top choice for AI development and examine the core services you'll be using throughout this book. The journey into AI on Azure begins with setting up the right environment—and ensuring you understand the tools at your disposal.

Why Azure for AI Development?

Microsoft Azure has emerged as one of the premier cloud platforms for developing, training, deploying, and managing Artificial Intelligence (AI) applications. With an integrated suite of services, global reach, and enterprise-grade capabilities, Azure offers a uniquely comprehensive environment that caters to AI practitioners across the entire spectrum—from startups and students to Fortune 500 companies and government organizations.

Azure's strength lies not only in its breadth of services, but also in the way those services interoperate to support the AI development lifecycle. Whether you are building predictive analytics models, computer vision systems, conversational agents, or real-time translation apps, Azure provides the tools and infrastructure to make it possible—efficiently, securely, and at scale.

Comprehensive AI Ecosystem

Azure's AI portfolio is vast and organized into multiple service layers to cater to a wide variety of use cases:

- **Pre-built Cognitive Services**: APIs for vision, speech, language, and decision-making.

- **Custom Model Training**: Azure Machine Learning for building, training, and deploying models.

- **Big Data Integration**: Azure Synapse Analytics, Data Lake, and Data Factory for handling massive datasets.

- **Deployment Services**: Kubernetes Service, Container Instances, Functions, and Logic Apps for hosting AI workloads.

- **Developer Tooling**: SDKs in Python, Java, C#, JavaScript, Jupyter Notebooks, and VS Code extensions.

This layered approach means you can begin with high-level tools and gradually move toward more granular, custom development as your needs evolve.

First-Class Tooling for Developers and Data Scientists

Azure is built with developers and data scientists in mind. It supports multiple popular programming languages, integrates with open-source ML/DL frameworks, and provides tooling designed for collaborative workflows.

With Azure Machine Learning (AzureML), users can:

- Create and manage compute clusters

- Schedule and track experiments

- Perform   AutoML

- Conduct   Responsible   AI   assessments

- Deploy   models   as   RESTful   web   services

For instance, a Python developer can quickly set up an experiment with the AzureML SDK:

```
from azureml.core import Workspace, Experiment, ScriptRunConfig

ws = Workspace.from_config()
experiment = Experiment(workspace=ws, name='my-first-ai-experiment')

config = ScriptRunConfig(source_directory='./scripts',
                         script='train.py',
                         compute_target='cpu-cluster')

run = experiment.submit(config)
run.wait_for_completion(show_output=True)
```

These streamlined workflows reduce friction in model development and increase productivity, especially in team-based environments.

Seamless Integration with DevOps and MLOps

Modern AI projects go beyond data science—they involve CI/CD pipelines, testing, monitoring, rollback strategies, and governance. Azure integrates seamlessly with Azure DevOps, GitHub Actions, and third-party tools to support MLOps practices out of the box.

You can:

- Trigger   model   training   on   pull   requests

- Deploy   containers   via   Azure   Pipelines

- Use   GitHub   repositories   to   version   data   and   models

- Monitor   model   drift   and   retrain   with   Azure   ML   Pipelines

```
# GitHub Actions: Trigger Azure ML training on code commit
name: Train Model

on:
```

```
push:
  paths:
    - 'models/**'

jobs:
  build:
    runs-on: ubuntu-latest
    steps:
    - name: Checkout code
      uses: actions/checkout@v2
    - name: Azure Login
      uses: azure/login@v1
      with:
        creds: ${{ secrets.AZURE_CREDENTIALS }}
    - name: Run training job
      run: |
        az ml job create --file models/training-job.yaml
```

This operational excellence ensures that AI doesn't live in a silo, but becomes a well-integrated, governed component of your software delivery pipeline.

Enterprise-Ready Security and Compliance

Security and compliance are foundational to AI development, especially in industries like healthcare, finance, and government. Azure provides an enterprise-grade security posture that includes:

- **Role-Based Access Control (RBAC)**
- **Private Link and VNET integrations**
- **Customer-Managed Keys with Azure Key Vault**
- **Identity federation with Azure AD B2C**
- **Comprehensive audit trails via Azure Monitor and Log Analytics**

Azure also maintains over 90 compliance certifications globally, including HIPAA, ISO 27001, FedRAMP, and GDPR, making it one of the most compliant cloud platforms available.

For example, securing AI endpoints can be as simple as:

```
# Restrict public access and integrate with VNET
az ml online-endpoint update --name sentiment-endpoint \
```

```
--set traffic=0 \
--set public_network_access=Disabled
```

This helps ensure that sensitive data used in AI workloads remains protected at all times.

Responsible AI Tooling

One of Azure's standout features is its built-in support for **Responsible AI**. Through both automated tools and manual guidelines, Azure allows developers to evaluate and improve model fairness, explainability, privacy, and robustness.

You can use the **Responsible AI dashboard** within AzureML to:

- Visualize feature importance

- Detect data imbalance or bias

- Analyze model error rates across subgroups

- Interpret individual predictions using SHAP and LIME

Additionally, the `azureml-interpret` SDK enables in-code generation of these insights:

```python
from interpret.ext.blackbox import TabularExplainer

explainer = TabularExplainer(model,
                             X_train,
                             features=X_train.columns,
                             classes=['yes', 'no'])

global_explanation = explainer.explain_global(X_test)
global_explanation.visualize()
```

This ensures your AI systems are not only performant but also accountable.

Cost-Effective Scalability

Azure gives you fine-grained control over your infrastructure, allowing you to match your AI resource needs with your budget. With features like auto-scaling, reserved instances, and spot pricing, you can optimize compute costs at every stage of the development lifecycle.

You can deploy a model to a CPU instance for testing and scale up to GPU-backed Kubernetes clusters for production with just a few changes in your deployment spec:

```
compute:
  instance_type: Standard_NC6
  min_instances: 1
  max_instances: 5
autoscale:
  enabled: true
```

Tools like Azure Cost Management + Billing let you forecast and control AI project expenditures down to the resource level, giving teams full visibility and control.

Hybrid and Edge AI Flexibility

Not every AI workload lives solely in the cloud. Some applications require edge deployment for low-latency, disconnected environments—such as factory automation, retail analytics, or healthcare diagnostics. Azure offers robust support for **Hybrid and Edge AI** through:

- **Azure Arc**: Extend Azure ML services to on-prem environments

- **IoT Edge + ML**: Deploy models to edge devices with containerization

- **Azure Stack**: Run full AI pipelines on local infrastructure

A typical edge deployment flow might involve:

1. Training a model in AzureML

2. Converting it to ONNX format

3. Packaging it as a Docker container

4. Deploying to an IoT Edge device using the Azure IoT Hub

```
az ml model convert --name mymodel \
                --target-format onnx

az iot edge deploy --device-id edgeDevice1 \
                --config deployment.json
```

This level of flexibility ensures that AI can go wherever it is needed, without being bound by cloud-only constraints.

Global Reach with Local Impact

Azure spans **more than 60 regions globally**, ensuring that AI services are available close to users and data sources. This reduces latency, ensures data sovereignty, and improves user experience for AI-powered applications across the globe.

Each region also offers redundancy and failover capabilities, ensuring high availability and resilience of critical AI services. This is especially important in mission-critical applications like real-time translation for emergency services or predictive maintenance in industrial settings.

A Platform with Momentum

Microsoft continuously invests in AI research, open-source collaboration, and product innovation. Azure customers benefit from:

- **Ongoing integration of new AI models (e.g., OpenAI's GPT series)**

- **Enterprise-grade   support   and   SLAs**

- **Tutorials,   certifications,   and   learning   paths**

- **A   vibrant   community   of   developers   and   researchers**

This ensures that Azure remains a forward-looking platform, enabling you to keep pace with AI innovation without constantly changing your technology stack.

In conclusion, Azure is not just a cloud provider with AI capabilities—it is a **strategically designed AI development platform**. With its full-stack integration, responsible AI tools, flexible deployment options, and enterprise-grade support, Azure enables developers and data scientists to move from prototype to production with confidence.

Choosing Azure for your AI development means leveraging the collective experience, security, and global infrastructure of one of the world's largest technology providers. As we move deeper into this book, we'll explore how to set up your Azure environment and start putting these powerful tools into action.

Key Azure Services for AI Applications

Microsoft Azure provides a vast and continually evolving array of cloud-based services designed to support the full AI application lifecycle. These services enable you to ingest, process, analyze, and act on data using intelligent models. In this section, we will explore the core Azure services that form the foundation for modern AI applications, categorized across five functional domains: data, model building, deployment, orchestration, and observability.

Azure's AI capabilities are not siloed; they are tightly integrated with its general-purpose cloud infrastructure, allowing AI systems to operate at scale, comply with security and governance policies, and connect to virtually any data source or application.

Azure Cognitive Services

Azure Cognitive Services is a family of pre-trained, REST-based AI APIs that enable developers to easily add intelligent features to their applications. These services are organized into several categories:

Vision

These APIs allow you to process and understand images and videos.

- **Computer Vision**: Extract text, identify objects, and generate image descriptions.

- **Face API**: Detect faces, recognize individuals, and analyze facial attributes (age, emotion, pose).

- **Form Recognizer**: Analyze and extract data from documents like invoices and receipts.

```
# Sample API call to analyze an image using Computer Vision
curl            -X            POST            "https://<your-
region>.api.cognitive.microsoft.com/vision/v3.2/analyze?visualFeatur
es=Description,Tags" \
    -H "Ocp-Apim-Subscription-Key: <your-key>" \
    -H "Content-Type: application/json" \
    --data '{"url":"https://example.com/image.jpg"}'
```

Speech

Includes services for converting speech to text, text to speech, and voice authentication.

- **Speech-to-Text**: Transcribe spoken words in real-time or from audio files.
- **Text-to-Speech**: Convert text into natural-sounding voice output.
- **Speaker Recognition**: Identify and verify users based on voice.

Language

These APIs deal with textual understanding and translation.

- **Text Analytics**: Sentiment analysis, entity recognition, language detection.
- **Translator**: Real-time translation between over 90 languages.

- **Language Understanding (LUIS)**: Build custom NLP models to understand user intentions.

Decision

Use AI to make informed decisions.

- **Personalizer**: Deliver personalized content based on reinforcement learning.

- **Content Moderator**: Detect offensive content in text, images, and videos.

- **Anomaly Detector**: Automatically detect unusual patterns in time-series data.

Search

Powered by Bing, these services allow intelligent search capabilities within apps.

• **Bing**	**Custom**	**Search**
• **Bing**	**Visual**	**Search**
• **Bing**	**News**	**Search**

These APIs help reduce time-to-market and eliminate the need for large datasets or training.

Azure Machine Learning (AzureML)

For custom AI model development, Azure Machine Learning is the cornerstone service. It supports the entire ML lifecycle:

• **Data**	**prep**	**and**	**labeling**
• **Model**	**training**	**and**	**tuning**
• **Model**	**deployment**	**and**	**monitoring**
• **MLOps**	**with**	**CI/CD**	**integration**

Core Features

- **Designer**: Drag-and-drop no-code interface.
- **Automated ML**: Auto-train and select the best model.

- **Python SDK**: Programmatic control over experiments and deployments.

- **Compute Clusters**: Scale on-demand with GPU/CPU-backed nodes.

- **Model Registry**: Version control for models.

- **Responsible AI Dashboards**: Visual tools to assess fairness, explainability, and privacy.

```
# Registering a model using AzureML SDK
from azureml.core import Workspace, Model

ws = Workspace.from_config()

model = Model.register(workspace=ws,
                       model_path="outputs/model.pkl",
                       model_name="fraud-detector",
                       tags={"area": "finance"},
                       description="Detects          fraudulent
transactions")
```

AzureML also supports integration with Git, Jupyter, Docker, Kubernetes, and ONNX, making it one of the most versatile AI platforms in the cloud.

Azure Databricks

Databricks is a unified data analytics platform built on Apache Spark and optimized for Azure. It is particularly effective for big data workloads, collaborative notebooks, and model training at scale.

Use cases include:

- **Distributed model training**

- **Data engineering and feature pipelines**

- **Real-time analytics with streaming data**

- **ETL and batch inference**

Azure Databricks provides high concurrency, auto-scaling clusters, and direct integration with Azure Blob Storage, Data Lake, and SQL Database.

```
# Spark example for data transformation
```

```
df    =    spark.read.csv("/mnt/data/clean_data.csv",    header=True,
inferSchema=True)
df = df.withColumn("risk_score", df["amount"] * 0.05)
df.write.format("delta").save("/mnt/data/risk_scores")
```

This allows seamless handoff between data engineering and data science teams.

Azure Data Services

AI applications are data-hungry. Azure provides a rich set of data services to ingest, transform, and store massive volumes of structured and unstructured data.

- **Azure Data Lake Storage**: Petabyte-scale storage for analytics.

- **Azure SQL Database**: Relational DB with ML integration.

- **Cosmos DB**: Globally distributed NoSQL database with millisecond latency.

- **Azure Synapse Analytics**: Combine big data and data warehousing for deep analytics.

- **Azure Data Factory**: ETL service for building data pipelines.

For example, a data pipeline for model training may involve:

1. Extracting customer data from Cosmos DB.

2. Transforming it using Data Factory.

3. Storing features in Data Lake.

4. Training the model with AzureML.

```
{
  "name": "TrainingDataPipeline",
  "activities": [
    {
      "name": "CopyCustomerData",
      "type": "Copy",
      "source": { "type": "CosmosDbSource" },
      "sink": { "type": "AzureBlobSink" }
    }
  ]
}
```

```
}
```

This flexibility supports AI at scale and meets compliance for data governance.

Azure Kubernetes Service (AKS)

For scalable deployment of AI models, AKS allows you to containerize and orchestrate services with high availability and fault tolerance.

- Deploy ML models as microservices.
- Use GPU-backed nodes for inference.
- Implement A/B testing and blue-green deployments.
- Auto-scale with load-based triggers.

```yaml
apiVersion: apps/v1
kind: Deployment
metadata:
  name: fraud-detector-deployment
spec:
  replicas: 3
  template:
    spec:
      containers:
      - name: fraud-detector
        image: myregistry.azurecr.io/fraud-detector:latest
        ports:
        - containerPort: 5000
```

With Azure ML, you can even create Kubernetes-based inference endpoints with just a few lines of code using the Python SDK or CLI.

Azure Functions and Logic Apps

For serverless workflows and event-driven AI applications, Azure Functions and Logic Apps enable integration without infrastructure management.

- Trigger ML inference on file uploads or API calls.
- Send data to AzureML from external services.

- Orchestrate pipelines with minimal code.

```
import logging
import json
import azure.functions as func

def main(req: func.HttpRequest) -> func.HttpResponse:
    data = json.loads(req.get_body())
    prediction = call_model(data)
    return func.HttpResponse(json.dumps({"prediction": prediction}),
status_code=200)
```

Serverless options are ideal for low-volume, infrequent AI tasks that need cost-efficiency and elasticity.

Azure OpenAI Service

Microsoft's partnership with OpenAI brings large-scale generative models to Azure users. You can access:

- **GPT-4** for text generation
- **DALL·E** for image creation
- **Whisper** for speech-to-text transcription
- **Codex** for code generation

Use cases include:

- Intelligent chatbots
- Code assistants
- Content summarization
- Translation and localization
- Prompt-based learning

```
import openai

openai.api_base = "https://<your-resource-name>.openai.azure.com/"
```

```
openai.api_key = "<your-key>"

response = openai.ChatCompletion.create(
    deployment_id="gpt-4",
    messages=[
        {"role": "system", "content": "You are a helpful assistant."},
        {"role": "user", "content": "Summarize this product review."}
    ]
)

print(response.choices[0].message["content"])
```

With built-in support for responsible use and pricing controls, the Azure OpenAI Service empowers you to add LLM capabilities to production applications.

In summary, Azure's suite of AI services is built to be comprehensive, extensible, and ready for enterprise use. Whether you need a pre-trained API to embed quickly into an app, or a fully custom ML model running in a hybrid Kubernetes environment, Azure has the services and scalability to support your needs.

The next section will explore the target audience for these services and outline the learning objectives for the remainder of the book, helping you understand how best to navigate this powerful ecosystem and apply it to your own AI projects.

Target Audience and Learning Objectives

Azure's AI ecosystem is vast, flexible, and powerful. But for those new to it—or even to AI itself—the breadth of tools and technologies can feel overwhelming. This book is designed to guide a diverse range of readers through the process of understanding, building, and deploying AI applications on Azure. To that end, it's critical to define who this book is for and what readers can expect to gain by the time they complete it.

Who This Book is For

AI on Azure isn't limited to researchers or seasoned developers. Microsoft has carefully designed its services to support a variety of skill levels and roles, each with their own objectives. Below are some of the key audiences that this book caters to.

Developers and Software Engineers

Developers are often the first to prototype and build AI-powered applications. They may not be deeply involved in the training of machine learning models, but they are responsible for embedding intelligent features into web, mobile, or desktop applications.

Use Cases:

- Integrating Azure Cognitive Services into apps for speech recognition or object detection.

- Embedding chatbots using Azure Bot Services.

- Connecting serverless triggers (Azure Functions) to AI predictions.

Skills Gained:

- Calling REST APIs to consume pre-trained AI models.

- Connecting apps to Azure ML endpoints.

- Handling input/output data formats (JSON, binary, text, etc.).

- Performing client-side validation and performance optimization.

Data Scientists and Machine Learning Engineers

These professionals focus on building, tuning, and validating predictive models using structured and unstructured data. They typically rely on platforms like Azure Machine Learning for experimentation and deployment.

Use Cases:

- Training a classification model to detect fraudulent financial transactions.

- Using AutoML to select the best regression model for real estate price prediction.

- Deploying NLP models for sentiment analysis in call center feedback.

Skills Gained:

- Preprocessing and analyzing data using Python and Azure notebooks.

- Performing feature engineering and model evaluation.

- Managing datasets and experiments using the AzureML SDK.

- Deploying and versioning models as endpoints for consumption.

```
from azureml.core import Dataset
```

```
# Load a dataset from registered resources
dataset = Dataset.get_by_name(ws, name='training-data')
df = dataset.to_pandas_dataframe()

# Begin preprocessing
df['amount_scaled'] = df['amount'] / df['amount'].max()
```

DevOps and MLOps Engineers

MLOps is an emerging discipline combining software engineering, machine learning, and operations. Engineers in this role ensure that AI models can be continuously trained, deployed, monitored, and updated.

Use Cases:

- Automating retraining pipelines triggered by new data in Azure Blob Storage.

- Creating CI/CD pipelines using Azure DevOps and GitHub Actions.

- Setting up model drift alerts and retraining triggers.

Skills Gained:

- Building training pipelines with Azure ML Pipelines.

- Connecting model deployment with Azure Kubernetes Service.

- Logging and monitoring model performance over time.

- Managing secrets, keys, and access using Azure Key Vault and RBAC.

```
# Sample GitHub Actions pipeline snippet
jobs:
  deploy_model:
    runs-on: ubuntu-latest
    steps:
    - uses: actions/checkout@v2
    - name: Login to Azure
      uses: azure/login@v1
      with:
        creds: ${{ secrets.AZURE_CREDENTIALS }}
    - name: Deploy Model
```

```
run: az ml online-endpoint deploy --name my-endpoint --model-id
mymodel:1
```

AI Enthusiasts and Students

Azure's intuitive interfaces, low-barrier services, and generous free-tier make it an excellent playground for learners. Whether you're a student enrolled in a machine learning course or a self-taught enthusiast, Azure lets you experiment safely and affordably.

Use Cases:

- Performing image classification using a Jupyter notebook and preloaded dataset.

- Building a speech-to-text demo app with minimal coding.

- Exploring Responsible AI using the built-in dashboards.

Skills Gained:

- Understanding the building blocks of AI systems.

- Creating simple models without extensive programming.

- Learning about model fairness, bias, and transparency.

- Exploring sample datasets and best practices.

Enterprise Architects and Decision Makers

Executives, architects, and solution designers often need to understand the strategic value and technical implications of AI without writing code. They design system architectures and make decisions about tooling, scalability, governance, and compliance.

Use Cases:

- Choosing the right mix of Azure services for a multi-tenant AI system.

- Ensuring compliance with GDPR, HIPAA, and other regulations.

- Selecting cloud regions for latency-sensitive deployments.

- Budgeting and forecasting for compute-heavy AI workflows.

Skills Gained:

- High-level understanding of service architecture.

- Tradeoffs between SaaS, PaaS, and IaaS for AI solutions.

- Understanding pricing models and optimizing cost-performance.

- Evaluating risk in AI adoption.

Learning Objectives

Regardless of your background or role, this book aims to empower you with the knowledge and skills necessary to confidently work with Azure AI tools. By the end of this book, you should be able to:

1. Set Up a Productive AI Development Environment

- Create and configure an Azure account.

- Understand the Azure Portal, CLI, and Resource Manager.

- Choose the right development tools: VS Code, Notebooks, AzureML Studio.

2. Understand and Utilize Azure's AI Services

- Differentiate between pre-trained APIs (Cognitive Services) and custom ML models (AzureML).

- Connect Azure AI services to real-world applications using SDKs or REST APIs.

- Identify appropriate services for vision, language, speech, and decision-making tasks.

3. Build and Deploy Custom Machine Learning Models

- Prepare data, conduct feature engineering, and visualize insights.

- Train, tune, and evaluate models using AzureML Designer and Python SDK.

- Deploy models as real-time inference endpoints or batch scoring jobs.

```python
# Example: Deploying a model as an endpoint
from azureml.core.model import InferenceConfig
from azureml.core.webservice import AciWebservice
```

```
inference_config        =        InferenceConfig(entry_script='score.py',
environment=myenv)

deployment_config = AciWebservice.deploy_configuration(cpu_cores=1,
memory_gb=1)

service = Model.deploy(workspace=ws,
                       name='predictor-endpoint',
                       models=[model],
                       inference_config=inference_config,
                       deployment_config=deployment_config)

service.wait_for_deployment(show_output=True)
```

4. Integrate AI Models into Full Applications

- Create AI-powered web, mobile, and desktop applications using Azure-hosted endpoints.

- Use Azure Functions and Logic Apps to automate workflows and data processing.

- Understand latency, scaling, and network considerations in real-time inference.

5. Implement Secure and Compliant AI Workflows

- Use RBAC, private endpoints, and Azure Key Vault for access control.

- Track, monitor, and log activities using Azure Monitor and Application Insights.

- Evaluate models using Responsible AI tools to ensure fairness and transparency.

6. Optimize and Scale AI Applications

- Monitor resource utilization and cost metrics.

- Use autoscaling and AKS for production-grade deployment.

- Use spot pricing, reserved instances, and tiered storage to manage costs.

7. Explore Real-World Use Cases and Architectures

- Analyze case studies from healthcare, retail, manufacturing, and finance.

- Learn hybrid deployment strategies using Azure Arc and IoT Edge.

- Understand enterprise patterns for governance and lifecycle management.

Prerequisites

To get the most out of this book, readers should ideally have:

- A basic understanding of programming (preferably in Python or JavaScript).

- Familiarity with fundamental AI/ML concepts (classification, regression, etc.).

- An Azure account (free or paid) for following along with hands-on examples.

- Willingness to explore, experiment, and apply best practices.

For readers without a technical background, the early chapters are designed to ramp up knowledge gradually, while later chapters offer deeper dives into implementation.

By aligning with the needs of these audiences and setting clear learning objectives, this book aims to be a practical and adaptable resource. Whether your goal is to deploy your first AI model, integrate speech recognition into an app, or evaluate architecture choices for a hybrid deployment, you will find the guidance, code, and context you need to succeed with Azure AI.

In the next chapter, we will move into setting up your Azure AI environment, covering how to create an account, use the CLI, configure services, and apply best practices for a solid foundation.

Chapter 2: Setting Up Your Azure AI Environment

Creating and Configuring Your Azure Account

Before you can begin building AI solutions with Microsoft Azure, you must first establish a solid foundation by setting up and configuring your Azure environment. This involves more than simply creating an account—it means setting up proper authentication, organizing your resources, choosing appropriate service tiers, and enabling essential tools for development and deployment. In this section, we will walk through each step in detail to ensure your environment is secure, scalable, and ready for AI workloads.

Creating an Azure Account

Azure offers a generous free tier for new users, including access to select services for 12 months, a $200 credit for the first 30 days, and always-free services like Azure Functions, App Services, and Cosmos DB with limited quotas.

Steps to Create an Account

1. **Go** **to** https://azure.microsoft.com
2. Click on **Start** **free** or **Free** **account**.
3. Sign in with a Microsoft account or create one.
4. Verify your identity using a phone number and a valid credit card.
5. Agree to the terms and complete the sign-up.

Once signed up, you'll be taken to the **Azure Portal**, your web-based management interface for all Azure resources.

Understanding Azure Subscriptions and Tenants

- **Subscription**: A billing container for resources. All your services are tied to a subscription, which can have its own spending limits and role-based access control (RBAC).

- **Tenant**: A dedicated instance of Azure Active Directory (Azure AD). It governs identity and access.

You can have multiple subscriptions under one tenant, allowing for separation of environments (e.g., Dev, QA, Production) while maintaining centralized identity management.

```
# List all subscriptions using Azure CLI
az account list --output table

# Set a specific subscription as active
az account set --subscription "My Subscription Name"
```

Installing and Configuring the Azure CLI

While the Azure Portal is user-friendly, using the CLI increases speed and enables automation. Azure CLI is cross-platform and scriptable, ideal for repetitive tasks and CI/CD pipelines.

Installation

- **Windows**: Use the installer from the official site.

- **macOS**: brew install azure-cli

- **Linux**: Use package managers like apt or yum depending on your distro.

First Time Login

```
az login
```

This command opens a browser window to log in. After authenticating, your CLI session is connected to your Azure account.

Creating a Resource Group

A **Resource Group** is a logical container for resources like storage accounts, virtual machines, or ML services.

```
az group create --name ai-projects --location eastus
```

You should create separate resource groups for each project or environment. This allows for easier cost tracking, access control, and cleanup.

Setting Up Your AI Tooling

To build AI applications, you'll use a combination of local tools and Azure-hosted services. Below are the key tools to install and configure.

Visual Studio Code (VS Code)

VS Code is the most popular code editor for Azure development. Install these extensions:

- **Azure**   **Account**

- **Azure**   **ML**

- **Python**

- **Docker**

Azure Machine Learning Extension

This allows you to manage and deploy ML models directly from your editor. Once installed, you can browse workspaces, view registered models, and run experiments.

Python Environment

Ensure you have Python 3.8+ installed along with the `azureml-sdk`:

```
pip install azureml-sdk
```

Optional but recommended:

```
pip install jupyter pandas scikit-learn matplotlib
```

Jupyter notebooks are often used for data analysis, model training, and experimentation.

Provisioning Azure Machine Learning Workspace

The AzureML workspace is a centralized place to manage compute resources, datasets, models, and experiments.

```
az ml workspace create --name ai-lab --resource-group ai-projects --location eastus
```

Alternatively, use Python:

```python
from azureml.core import Workspace

ws = Workspace.create(name='ai-lab',
                      subscription_id='your-subscription-id',
                      resource_group='ai-projects',
                      location='eastus',
                      create_resource_group=True,
                      exist_ok=True)
```

```
ws.write_config(path='.azureml')
```

Once the workspace is set up, you can begin registering datasets, training models, and deploying endpoints.

Configuring Compute Resources

AI workloads are compute-intensive. Azure provides multiple compute targets:

- **Compute Instances**: For development, debugging, and interactive notebook use.

- **Compute Clusters**: For batch training at scale, with autoscaling.

- **Inference Clusters**: For deploying models in production.

Create a compute instance from the CLI:

```
az ml compute create --name dev-instance \
                     --type ComputeInstance \
                     --size Standard_DS3_v2 \
                     --workspace-name ai-lab \
                     --resource-group ai-projects
```

For cluster creation:

```
az ml compute create --name train-cluster \
                     --type AmlCompute \
                     --min-instances 0 \
                     --max-instances 4 \
                     --size Standard_NC6
```

Setting Up Networking and Security

Security should be considered from day one.

Role-Based Access Control (RBAC)

Assign roles to users at the subscription, resource group, or resource level.

```
az role assignment create \
  --assignee "<user-email>" \
  --role "Contributor" \
  --resource-group "ai-projects"
```

Virtual Networks (VNET)

Create a virtual network to isolate traffic between AI services and other Azure components.

Key Vault

Secure API keys, passwords, and certificates.

```
az keyvault create --name ai-vault --resource-group ai-projects --
location eastus

az keyvault secret set --vault-name ai-vault --name
"CognitiveServiceKey" --value "your-api-key"
```

You can access this secret in your Python code:

```python
from azure.identity import DefaultAzureCredential
from azure.keyvault.secrets import SecretClient

credential = DefaultAzureCredential()
client = SecretClient(vault_url="https://ai-vault.vault.azure.net/",
credential=credential)

secret = client.get_secret("CognitiveServiceKey")
print(secret.value)
```

Using Azure Notebooks

Azure provides hosted Jupyter notebooks for data scientists who want to work directly in the cloud without local configuration.

To enable:

1. Go to your ML Workspace in the Azure Portal.

2. Select **Notebooks** from the sidebar.

3. Create or connect a compute instance.

4. Start writing and running notebooks directly in the browser.

Azure Notebooks are version-controlled, support Git integration, and are tightly integrated with datasets and models stored in the workspace.

Organizing Your Project Structure

To manage complexity, structure your codebase and infrastructure:

```
/ai-project/
|
├── data/
├── notebooks/
├── models/
├── pipelines/
├── .azureml/
├── environment.yml
├── requirements.txt
└── README.md
```

This layout supports reproducibility and team collaboration. You can also integrate with Azure DevOps or GitHub for source control and CI/CD.

Automating Resource Setup with ARM Templates or Bicep

Azure Resource Manager (ARM) templates allow for declarative infrastructure provisioning. Bicep is a simplified DSL for writing ARM templates.

Example Bicep for creating a resource group and ML workspace:

```
resource rg 'Microsoft.Resources/resourceGroups@2021-04-01' = {
  name: 'ai-projects'
  location: 'eastus'
}

resource                                              workspace
'Microsoft.MachineLearningServices/workspaces@2023-04-01' = {
  name: 'ai-lab'
  location: 'eastus'
  properties: {
    description: 'AI lab workspace'
  }
}
```

Deploy with:

```
az deployment sub create --location eastus --template-file main.bicep
```

Best Practices Summary

- Use a dedicated resource group per environment or project.

- Keep secrets in Azure Key Vault—not in source code.

- Enable logging and monitoring from day one.

- Separate development and production workspaces.

- Automate resource creation to maintain consistency.

Setting up your Azure AI environment is a foundational step that sets the tone for everything that follows. By organizing resources, installing tools, and configuring security and automation, you ensure that your AI projects are secure, repeatable, and scalable from the very beginning.

In the next section, we'll explore how to navigate the Azure Portal and CLI more effectively, giving you the skills to manage your AI infrastructure with confidence and speed.

Navigating the Azure Portal and CLI

Effectively using Azure for AI development requires familiarity with both the Azure Portal and the Azure Command-Line Interface (CLI). These two interfaces serve different, complementary roles in managing and deploying cloud-based resources. The Portal offers a graphical, interactive experience, while the CLI allows for automation, scripting, and bulk operations. Together, they empower developers, data scientists, and administrators to work efficiently and consistently.

In this section, we will explore both tools in detail—starting with the Azure Portal, progressing to CLI usage, and finishing with advanced navigation and scripting techniques that will help streamline your AI development workflow.

The Azure Portal: Visual Control of Your Cloud Resources

The Azure Portal is the web-based interface where you can manage your Azure resources, configure services, monitor usage, and access visual tools for creating and managing AI workflows.

Accessing the Portal

Visit: https://portal.azure.com

After logging in, you'll be presented with the **Dashboard**. This is a customizable layout that can include your most-used services, pinned resources, charts, cost estimates, and more.

You can create a new dashboard or customize the default one by:

1. Clicking **Dashboard** from the left menu.

2. Selecting **New Dashboard**.

3. Dragging and dropping resources, charts, and widgets from the gallery.

Key Areas of the Portal

- **Home**: A launchpad to common tasks and recently used services.

- **All Services**: A searchable directory of every Azure service.

- **Resource Groups**: Logical containers for managing collections of resources.

- **Subscriptions**: View and switch between multiple billing accounts.

- **AI + Machine Learning**: Shortcut to AzureML Studio, Cognitive Services, Bot Services, and more.

Creating Resources via the Portal

To create a resource:

1. Click **Create a Resource** on the top-left.

2. Select a category like "AI + Machine Learning".

3. Choose a specific service (e.g., Azure Machine Learning).

4. Follow the wizard to fill in configuration options: resource group, region, pricing tier, etc.

This approach is ideal for first-time users who want to visually explore configurations and see immediate feedback.

Managing Machine Learning Workspaces

Once created, an AzureML workspace provides access to:

- **Datasets**: Upload and register files or connect to data stores.

- **Compute**: Manage your compute clusters and instances.

- **Experiments**: Monitor model training runs.

- **Pipelines**: Orchestrate multi-step ML workflows.

- **Models**: Register, version, and deploy your trained models.

- **Endpoints**: RESTful APIs for serving models in production.

Each section contains visual tools for management, such as running Jupyter notebooks, configuring environments, or tracking run metrics.

Portal Shortcuts and Productivity Tips

- Use **Global Search** (Ctrl + /) to find resources instantly.

- Click the **Cloud Shell** button at the top to launch an embedded terminal.

- Pin commonly used services to the left sidebar using the ellipsis (...) > **Pin to dashboard**.

- Use the **Activity Log** in resource groups to audit operations.

Azure CLI: Automating Your Workflow

While the Portal is intuitive, the CLI is essential for automating deployments, scripting repeatable tasks, and managing infrastructure programmatically.

Installing the Azure CLI

- **Windows**: Download the installer from the official Microsoft docs.

macOS: Use Homebrew:

```
brew install azure-cli
```

-

Linux: Use your package manager:

```
curl -sL https://aka.ms/InstallAzureCLIDeb | sudo bash
```

-

Initial Configuration

Login to Azure:

```
az login
```

This opens a browser for authentication. After logging in, the CLI caches your credentials.

To set the active subscription:

```
az account list --output table
az account set --subscription "My Subscription"
```

Set a default resource group and location:

```
az configure --defaults group=ai-projects location=eastus
```

This reduces the need to repeat parameters in every command.

Common CLI Operations for AI Projects

Creating a Resource Group

```
az group create --name ai-projects --location eastus
```

Creating an AzureML Workspace

```
az ml workspace create --name ai-lab --resource-group ai-projects --location eastus
```

Creating a Compute Cluster

```
az ml compute create --name cpu-cluster --size Standard_DS3_v2 --type AmlCompute --max-instances 4
```

Deploying a Model Endpoint

```
az ml online-endpoint create --name fraud-detector --file endpoint.yml
```

You can also update, delete, or scale these resources directly from the CLI.

Output Formatting and Querying

The CLI supports three output formats:

- `--output` table

- `--output` json

- `--output` yaml

Use the `--query` parameter with JMESPath expressions to filter results:

```
az group list --query "[?location=='eastus'].name" --output table
```

This is useful for scripting and integrating with other tools.

Cloud Shell: The Best of Both Worlds

Azure Cloud Shell is a browser-based terminal available directly within the Portal. It supports both Bash and PowerShell and comes pre-installed with:

- Azure CLI

- Git

- Python

- Terraform

- Docker

- kubectl

To launch it, click the **Cloud Shell** icon in the top menu bar of the Portal.

You can mount Azure Files as persistent storage and store scripts, datasets, or configuration files directly in the shell.

Combining Portal and CLI for Efficient Workflow

Many tasks in Azure can be approached through either the Portal or CLI. Here's when to use each:

Task	Use Portal	Use CLI
First-time resource creation	✓ Guided forms	⊘ Slower if unfamiliar with syntax

Scripting batch operations	⊘ Manual and repetitive	✓ Ideal for automation
Monitoring and logging	✓ Visual dashboards	✓ Can export and filter logs
Setting up dev environments	✓ Easy with wizards	✓ More control over config
Team collaboration	✓ Role management UI	✓ Scriptable via RBAC commands

By mastering both interfaces, you'll gain agility and confidence in managing everything from simple AI prototypes to production-grade, globally distributed AI systems.

Troubleshooting and Productivity Tips

- Use `az --help` or `az <command> --help` to get quick documentation.

- Install the Azure CLI Extensions like `ml`, `aks-preview`, or `ai-examples` to extend CLI functionality.

- Use Bash scripting or PowerShell to create automated provisioning scripts.

- Use `az feedback` to report bugs or suggest improvements directly to Microsoft.

Example: Full AI Project Setup Script

```bash
#!/bin/bash

# Set project variables
RG_NAME="ai-projects"
LOCATION="eastus"
WS_NAME="ai-lab"
CLUSTER_NAME="train-cluster"

# Create resource group
az group create --name $RG_NAME --location $LOCATION

# Create ML workspace
az ml workspace create --name $WS_NAME --resource-group $RG_NAME --location $LOCATION
```

```
# Create compute cluster
az ml compute create --name $CLUSTER_NAME --type AmlCompute --size
Standard_DS3_v2 --min-instances 0 --max-instances 4
```

Run this once, and your AI project environment is ready to use.

Mastering the Azure Portal and CLI allows you to navigate your AI development environment with confidence and precision. Whether you prefer visual workflows or command-line efficiency, both tools offer robust support for deploying, monitoring, and managing AI services in Azure.

In the next section, we'll explore how to leverage Azure DevOps to create repeatable, collaborative workflows for training, testing, and deploying AI models.

Using Azure DevOps for AI Projects

AI development isn't just about building models—it's about managing the entire lifecycle of data, experimentation, deployment, and ongoing maintenance. Azure DevOps provides a robust platform for managing this lifecycle through integrated tools for version control, CI/CD (Continuous Integration and Continuous Deployment), collaboration, infrastructure-as-code, testing, and more. For AI projects that need to be reproducible, scalable, and compliant with governance standards, Azure DevOps is an essential tool.

This section dives deep into how Azure DevOps can be used to support every stage of your AI project workflow—from setting up your repo to deploying models to production.

Why Azure DevOps for AI?

Azure DevOps helps unify the traditionally siloed worlds of data science and software engineering. With Azure DevOps, teams can:

- Version control code, notebooks, data schemas, and pipelines.

- Collaborate through work items, task boards, and pull requests.

- Automate testing, training, and deployment.

- Enforce governance and reproducibility via pipelines and environments.

- Track model versions alongside application versions.

These capabilities are critical for AI projects, where experiments must be repeatable, results verifiable, and deployments traceable.

Core Components of Azure DevOps

Azure DevOps is a suite of services:

- **Azure Repos**: Git repositories for version control.

- **Azure Pipelines**: CI/CD pipelines for automation.

- **Azure Boards**: Agile planning and task management.

- **Azure Artifacts**: Package management for Python, NuGet, npm, and Maven.

- **Azure Test Plans**: Manual and exploratory testing tools.

Let's explore how to set each of these up for an AI project.

Getting Started: Setting Up Your Project

Create a DevOps Organization and Project

1. Go to https://dev.azure.com

2. Sign in with your Microsoft account.

3. Create a new organization.

4. Create a new project named `ai-model-pipeline`.

Choose Git as the version control system and select Basic or Agile process for boards.

Using Azure Repos for Version Control

Azure Repos offers private Git repositories with features like branch policies, pull request templates, and CI integration.

Best Practices for AI Projects

Structure your repo to separate code, models, and configurations:

```
ai-project/
├── data/
├── notebooks/
```

```
├── models/
├── src/
├── .azure-pipelines/
├── requirements.txt
└── README.md
```

Add a `.gitignore` file to exclude large data and secrets:

```
__pycache__/
*.pyc
.env
data/
outputs/
```

Commit your training scripts, environment configuration, and scoring scripts:

```
git init
git remote add origin https://dev.azure.com/yourorg/ai-model-pipeline/_git/ai-model-pipeline
git add .
git commit -m "Initial commit"
git push -u origin master
```

Use **branches** for experimentation and **pull requests** for merging validated work into main branches.

Automating with Azure Pipelines

Pipelines in Azure DevOps allow you to automate model training, testing, and deployment.

YAML Pipeline Example for ML Training

Create a file at `.azure-pipelines/train.yml`:

```
trigger:
  branches:
    include:
      - main
```

```yaml
pool:
  vmImage: 'ubuntu-latest'

variables:
  pythonVersion: '3.8'

steps:
  - task: UsePythonVersion@0
    inputs:
      versionSpec: '$(pythonVersion)'

  - script: |
      python -m pip install --upgrade pip
      pip install -r requirements.txt
    displayName: 'Install dependencies'

  - script: |
      python src/train.py --epochs 10 --model outputs/model.pkl
    displayName: 'Train model'

  - task: PublishBuildArtifacts@1
    inputs:
      pathToPublish: 'outputs'
      artifactName: 'model'
```

Commit and push this YAML file, then connect your project to Azure DevOps Pipelines:

1. Go to your Azure DevOps Project.

2. Click **Pipelines** > **New**. **Pipeline**.

3. Select your repository and use the YAML file from your repo.

The pipeline will run whenever changes are pushed to the main branch, training the model and publishing it as an artifact.

Managing Experiments with Azure ML and DevOps

You can also trigger model training in Azure Machine Learning from DevOps using CLI commands in your pipeline:

```
- script: |
    az extension add -n ml
    az ml job create --file jobs/train-job.yml
  displayName: 'Run training job in Azure ML'
```

A `train-job.yml` might look like:

```
code: ./src
command: >-
  python     train.py     --data    ../data/train.csv     --model
./outputs/model.pkl
environment: azureml:AzureML-sklearn-0.24-ubuntu18.04-py37-cpu:1
compute: azureml:train-cluster
experiment_name: ai-experiments
```

This approach allows full integration between DevOps and your ML workspace.

Testing AI Code and Models

Testing in AI involves both unit testing and model evaluation. Add test steps to your pipeline:

```
- script: |
    pip install pytest
    pytest tests/
  displayName: 'Run unit tests'
```

Include model evaluation scripts that assert accuracy or other metrics:

```python
import pickle
from sklearn.metrics import accuracy_score
import pandas as pd

model = pickle.load(open("outputs/model.pkl", "rb"))
X_test = pd.read_csv("data/X_test.csv")
y_test = pd.read_csv("data/y_test.csv")

y_pred = model.predict(X_test)
accuracy = accuracy_score(y_test, y_pred)

assert accuracy > 0.85, f"Model accuracy too low: {accuracy}"
```

This ensures models don't regress in quality when retrained.

Deploying Models via Pipelines

To deploy a model as an Azure ML endpoint:

```
- script: |
    az   ml   model   register   --name   fraud-detector   --path
outputs/model.pkl
    az   ml   online-endpoint   create   --name   fraud-api   --file
deployment/endpoint.yml
  displayName: 'Deploy model endpoint'
```

Use infrastructure-as-code YAML files to control deployment and enforce consistency across environments (dev, staging, prod).

Managing Secrets with Azure Key Vault

Avoid storing secrets in your repository. Instead, use Azure Key Vault with pipeline variables:

```
variables:
  - group: ai-secrets

steps:
  - script: echo "Using secret: $(CognitiveServicesKey)"
```

Create a variable group in **Pipelines > Library**, and link it to a Key Vault.

Azure Boards: Tracking Work and Experiments

Azure Boards provides a Kanban-style interface to manage work items. You can:

- Link work items to Git commits and pull requests.
- Track bugs, features, and model improvement requests.
- Create sprints and assign work to data scientists or engineers.

Example work items for an AI project:

- Train new fraud model on March dataset.

- Test deployment on staging environment.

- Review feature importance from model v2.1.

Artifacts and Model Versioning

Use Azure Artifacts or the Azure ML Model Registry to manage versions of your models. Each time your pipeline produces a new model:

```
- task: PublishBuildArtifacts@1
  inputs:
    pathToPublish: 'outputs/model.pkl'
    artifactName: 'fraud-detector'
```

In Azure ML, these are versioned automatically. You can query them later for audit purposes or rollback.

Real-World MLOps Pipeline

1. Developer pushes code to repo.

2. Pipeline runs: installs deps, runs tests, trains model.

3. Model is evaluated and metrics are logged.

4. If metrics pass threshold, model is deployed.

5. Notifications are sent to team via Slack, Teams, or email.

6. Metrics are monitored post-deployment for drift.

Summary: Benefits of Azure DevOps for AI

Feature	Benefit

CI/CD Pipelines	Automate testing, training, deployment
Repos with Branch Policies	Enforce code review and version control
Boards and Work Items	Manage experiments and track progress
Integration with Azure ML	Launch jobs and monitor results programmatically
Secret Management via Key Vault	Keep credentials and API keys secure
Artifact Versioning	Track model evolution and support rollback

Azure DevOps transforms AI development into a collaborative, governed, and scalable process. With proper integration, your data science and engineering teams can iterate faster, deploy with confidence, and build production-grade AI systems that are resilient and maintainable.

In the next section, we'll explore best practices for managing your Azure AI environment, including naming conventions, resource tagging, cost controls, and organizational structures.

Best Practices for Environment Management

As AI projects grow in complexity, scale, and organizational impact, managing your Azure environment effectively becomes essential. Poorly managed environments can lead to resource sprawl, cost overruns, inconsistent deployments, security vulnerabilities, and compliance failures. On the other hand, a well-structured, policy-driven, and automated environment enables rapid innovation, collaboration, cost efficiency, and long-term maintainability.

This section explores the best practices for managing Azure AI environments, covering naming conventions, resource organization, tagging, cost management, access control, network configuration, monitoring, automation, and governance.

Consistent Naming Conventions

Using standardized naming conventions across resources makes your environment easier to navigate, automate, and audit. Azure resources often appear in lists, logs, graphs, and dashboards—so clarity and consistency are key.

Recommended Naming Structure

```
<project>-<env>-<resource-type>-<region>
```

Example:

- `fraud-prod-ml-ws-eus` → Fraud detection, production, ML workspace, East US

- `vision-dev-vm-west` → Vision project, development, VM, West US

Common Abbreviations

Resource Type	Abbreviation
Resource Group	rg
Virtual Network	vnet
Storage Account	st
Key Vault	kv
Machine Learning WS	ml-ws
Compute Cluster	cc

This helps avoid ambiguous names like `test123` or `temp-cluster`.

Resource Group Organization

Azure Resource Groups act as logical containers for managing resources. Proper use of resource groups simplifies access control, cost tracking, and resource lifecycle management.

Best Practices

- **One resource group per environment:** e.g., `project-dev-rg`, `project-prod-rg`.

- **Keep related resources together:** Group all ML resources, compute, storage, and networks for a single solution.

- **Use resource locks on critical groups:** Prevent accidental deletions using "CanNotDelete" or "ReadOnly" locks.

```
az lock create --name prevent-deletion \
          --lock-type CanNotDelete \
          --resource-group fraud-prod-rg
```

Resource Tagging

Tags are metadata key-value pairs applied to resources. They enable filtering, reporting, and cost tracking across resource types.

Tag Categories

- **Environment:** env=dev, env=prod

- **Owner:** owner=john.doe@company.com

- **Project:** project=vision-ai

- **Cost Center:** costcenter=AI123

- **Compliance:** data-type=pii, regulation=HIPAA

Example CLI Tag Command

```
az resource tag --tags project=vision-ai env=prod owner=alice \
  --ids $(az resource show --name vision-prod-ml-ws --resource-group
vision-prod-rg --query id --output tsv)
```

Implement policies to **enforce tags** using Azure Policy:

```
az policy assignment create --name require-tags \
  --policy "Require a tag on resources" \
  --params '{ "tagName": { "value": "project" } }'
```

Cost Management and Optimization

AI workloads can be expensive. Effective cost management ensures budgets are respected and unused resources are identified quickly.

Tools for Cost Management

- **Azure Cost Management + Billing**: Set budgets, view trends, analyze cost per resource/tag.

- **Azure Advisor**: Recommendations for underutilized VMs, overprovisioned clusters, and unused resources.

- **Pricing Calculator**: Estimate costs before provisioning.

- **Budgets and Alerts**: Automatically notify stakeholders when nearing budget limits.

Cost Management Practices

- **Use spot instances** for non-critical training tasks.

- **Auto-shutdown dev compute** at night and on weekends.

- **Auto-scale inference clusters** to match traffic patterns.

- **Assign quotas to teams** using Azure Cost Management.

```
az consumption budget create --amount 500 --category cost \
  --name ai-training-budget --time-grain monthly \
  --start-date 2025-01-01 --end-date 2025-12-31 \
  --resource-group ai-dev-rg
```

Access Control with RBAC

Azure uses Role-Based Access Control (RBAC) to manage user and service permissions. This ensures the principle of least privilege is enforced.

Common Roles

Role	Purpose
Owner	Full control, including permissions
Contributor	Full control but cannot assign roles
Reader	View-only access

Machine Learning Admin   Full control of Azure ML resources

Storage Blob Data Reader   Access to read from blob containers

Assigning Roles

```
az role assignment create \
  --assignee john.doe@company.com \
  --role "Contributor" \
  --resource-group fraud-dev-rg
```

Group-based access via Azure AD is preferred for scalability.

Secure Networking

AI solutions often use sensitive data. Network configuration is vital to ensure that data doesn't traverse the public internet unless necessary.

Best Practices

- **Private Endpoints**: Connect services like AzureML and Storage securely.

- **Virtual Networks (VNets)**: Place compute, web apps, and databases inside VNets.

- **Network Security Groups (NSGs)**: Limit traffic between subnets.

- **Service Endpoints**: Secure traffic from VNet to Azure services like SQL and Storage.

```
az network vnet create --name ai-vnet --resource-group ai-prod-rg \
  --address-prefix 10.0.0.0/16 --subnet-name ml-subnet --subnet-
prefix 10.0.1.0/24
```

Add compute targets and ML workspaces to private subnets with VNet integration for additional protection.

Monitoring and Logging

Proactive monitoring helps detect anomalies, performance issues, and security breaches early.

Tools and Services

- **Azure Monitor:** Central monitoring hub.

- **Application Insights:** Telemetry for web apps and APIs.

- **Log Analytics:** Advanced querying and dashboards.

- **AzureML Run Logs:** Track experiment metrics, errors, outputs.

Example: Enable Monitoring on an ML Endpoint

```
az ml online-endpoint update \
  --name fraud-endpoint \
  --set identity.type="SystemAssigned" \
        logging.mode="all"
```

Create alerts for failed jobs or abnormal model behavior using Azure Monitor alerts:

```
az monitor metrics alert create \
  --name "FailedRunsAlert" \
  --resource-group ai-prod-rg \
  --scopes <workspace-id> \
  --condition "total FailedRuns > 5" \
  --description "Alert on high failure rate"
```

Automation with Infrastructure as Code (IaC)

Consistency and reproducibility are crucial in AI environments. Automate infrastructure using:

- **ARM Templates:** Native JSON-based templates.

- **Bicep:** Simplified ARM language.

- **Terraform:** Popular multi-cloud IaC tool.

Example: Bicep Template for ML Workspace

```
resource                                           workspace
'Microsoft.MachineLearningServices/workspaces@2023-04-01' = {
  name: 'ml-workspace-prod'
  location: 'eastus'
  properties: {
```

```
    description: 'Production workspace'
    publicNetworkAccess: 'Disabled'
  }
}
```

Deploy with:

```
az deployment group create --resource-group ai-prod-rg --template-
file main.bicep
```

Use version control to track infrastructure changes, and link templates to CI/CD pipelines for continuous provisioning.

Environment Segmentation

Separate environments help prevent accidents and enable clean testing:

- **Dev**: For experimentation and development.
- **Test**: For QA and integration testing.
- **Staging**: Mirrors production for final validation.
- **Prod**: Live environment with strict controls.

Each should have:

- Its own resource group or subscription.
- Environment-specific secrets and configuration.
- Guardrails like stricter RBAC, locked resources, and monitoring in production.

Governance and Policy Enforcement

Azure Policy allows organizations to enforce standards and prevent misconfigurations.

Sample Policies

- Require tags on all resources.

- Restrict locations (e.g., avoid non-GDPR compliant regions).

- Prevent creation of unapproved VM sizes.

```
az policy assignment create \
  --policy "allowed-locations" \
  --params '{ "listOfAllowedLocations": { "value": ["eastus",
"westeurope"] } }' \
  --name "EnforceLocationPolicy"
```

Use **Blueprints** to deploy compliant environments with pre-configured networks, identities, and policies.

Documentation and Knowledge Management

Maintaining clear internal documentation is essential:

- Maintain a README in each repo explaining architecture, setup, and workflow.

- Use Azure DevOps Wiki, Confluence, or SharePoint for team-wide documentation.

- Document model metadata, metrics, and decisions (bias audits, evaluation results).

Include:

- Network   diagrams

- IAM   policies

- Cost   breakdowns

- Service   dependencies

- Data   governance   policies

Summary Checklist

Area	Best Practices Summary

Naming	Consistent, structured, and meaningful names
Resource Groups	Organize per project/environment, use locks
Tags	Tag all resources for cost, ownership, and compliance tracking
Cost Management	Use budgets, alerts, and Azure Advisor
RBAC	Assign minimal required roles, prefer group-based access
Networking	Use private endpoints, VNETs, NSGs
Monitoring	Enable logging and alerts on key metrics
Automation	Use Bicep, ARM, or Terraform for repeatable deployments
Segmentation	Separate dev/test/prod environments
Governance	Enforce policies with Azure Policy and Blueprints
Documentation	Maintain internal documentation and decision logs

By adopting these best practices, your Azure AI environment will be not only scalable and secure, but also easier to manage, audit, and collaborate within. These strategies lay the groundwork for building AI solutions that are production-ready, cost-efficient, and aligned with enterprise requirements.

In the next chapter, we'll move on to exploring Azure Cognitive Services, where you'll begin applying AI features like computer vision, language understanding, and speech synthesis with just a few lines of code.

Chapter 3: Leveraging Azure Cognitive Services

Overview of Cognitive Services

Azure Cognitive Services is a powerful suite of pre-built, AI-powered APIs that allow developers to easily incorporate sophisticated capabilities such as image analysis, facial recognition, natural language understanding, text translation, speech processing, and intelligent search into their applications—without the need for in-depth machine learning expertise.

These services are designed to democratize AI by providing RESTful APIs and SDKs that work across programming languages, making it possible to bring AI features to production quickly and cost-effectively. In this section, we will explore the core principles behind Cognitive Services, how they are organized, and how they fit into AI application development workflows.

The Value Proposition of Cognitive Services

Traditionally, building AI solutions involved training models from scratch using custom data, which is time-consuming and requires significant domain expertise. With Cognitive Services, Microsoft has pre-trained models on massive datasets and made them accessible via simple API endpoints. This means developers and organizations can focus on integrating intelligence rather than building it from the ground up.

Key benefits include:

- **Ease of Use**: No machine learning background required.

- **Quick Integration**: Available through REST APIs and SDKs for Python, C#, JavaScript,   and   Java.

- **Scalability**: Backed by Azure infrastructure to scale globally.

- **Security and Compliance**: Built-in support for RBAC, Azure AD, and enterprise-grade SLAs.

- **Customization**: Many services support transfer learning and fine-tuning with your own data.

Categories of Azure Cognitive Services

Cognitive Services are divided into five broad categories, each targeting a specific domain of intelligence:

1. Vision

Enables your apps to analyze visual content in different ways:

- **Computer Vision**: Understand images, extract text (OCR), tag content, and generate descriptions.

- **Face API**: Detect and analyze faces, including emotion, age, and facial features.

- **Form Recognizer**: Extract structured data from forms, receipts, and invoices using machine learning.

- **Custom Vision**: Train your own image classifier on top of Microsoft's vision models.

2. Speech

Allows you to integrate real-time speech processing:

- **Speech to Text**: Transcribe spoken language into text.

- **Text to Speech**: Convert written text into spoken audio in many languages and styles.

- **Speaker Recognition**: Identify or verify users based on voice signatures.

- **Speech Translation**: Translate spoken audio into another language.

3. Language

Provides natural language processing capabilities:

- **Text Analytics**: Perform sentiment analysis, key phrase extraction, entity recognition, and language detection.

- **Language Understanding (LUIS)**: Create custom language models that recognize user intents.

- **Translator**: Translate text between 90+ languages in real time.

- **QnA Maker**: Create conversational Q&A layers over existing documents and web content.

4. Decision

Bring intelligent decision-making capabilities to your apps:

- **Personalizer**: Deliver personalized experiences using reinforcement learning.

- **Anomaly Detector**: Detect irregularities in time series data.

- **Content Moderator**: Detect offensive, unwanted, or risky content in text, images, and videos.

5. Search

Built on top of Bing APIs, these services enhance the discovery of information:

- **Bing Web Search**: Query the web for relevant documents, news, and images.

- **Bing Visual Search**: Search for similar images or products using an input image.

- **Bing Custom Search**: Build search engines tailored to specific content or websites.

Authentication and Access

To use any Cognitive Service, you first need to provision a resource on Azure:

1. Go to the **Azure Portal**.

2. Click **Create a resource > AI + Machine Learning > Cognitive Services**.

3. Select the resource type (e.g., Computer Vision), pricing tier, region, and resource group.

4. Once deployed, retrieve the **Endpoint** and **API Key** from the resource overview page.

These credentials are used to make authenticated API calls:

```
POST
https://<region>.api.cognitive.microsoft.com/vision/v3.2/analyze
Headers:
  Ocp-Apim-Subscription-Key: <your-api-key>
  Content-Type: application/json
Body:
{
  "url": "https://example.com/image.jpg"
}
```

Use Azure Key Vault to securely store and rotate your keys.

SDKs and Development Tools

Microsoft provides SDKs for multiple languages:

- **Python**: `pip install azure-cognitiveservices-vision-computervision`

- **C# (.NET)**: NuGet packages for each service

- **JavaScript**: npm packages like `@azure/cognitiveservices-computervision`

- **Java**: Maven dependencies for Java SDKs

These SDKs offer object-oriented access to each service and simplify integration.

Example: Using the Python SDK for Computer Vision

```python
from azure.cognitiveservices.vision.computervision import ComputerVisionClient
from msrest.authentication import CognitiveServicesCredentials

endpoint = "https://<region>.api.cognitive.microsoft.com"
key = "<your-api-key>"

client = ComputerVisionClient(endpoint, CognitiveServicesCredentials(key))

image_url = "https://example.com/image.jpg"
description = client.describe_image(image_url)
print(description.captions[0].text)
```

Deployment Models and Pricing

You can use Cognitive Services in two main deployment modes:

1. Multi-Tenant (Shared Infrastructure)

- Hosted by Microsoft.

- Simplest to use—just call the endpoint.

- Ideal for quick integration, testing, and most use cases.

2. Containerized Deployment (On-Prem/Edge)

- Use Docker containers for services like OCR, Face API, and Anomaly Detector.

- Supports disconnected or offline environments.

- Requires a license and metered billing via Azure.

```
docker pull mcr.microsoft.com/azure-cognitive-services/form-recognizer
docker run -it -p 5000:5000 mcr.microsoft.com/azure-cognitive-services/form-recognizer
```

Register usage with Azure by passing your API key during container startup.

Choosing the Right Services for Your Use Case

Use Case	Cognitive Service
Image content moderation	Content Moderator + Computer Vision
Speech-enabled chatbot	Speech to Text + LUIS + QnA Maker
Custom form processing	Form Recognizer (with labeled training)
News recommendation system	Bing News Search + Personalizer
Multi-language support for web apps	Translator + Language Detection
Detecting fraud in transactions	Anomaly Detector
Face-based identity verification	Face API + Speaker Recognition

Handling Data and Privacy

Cognitive Services process user data, often involving images, voices, and text. Microsoft provides:

- **GDPR** **Compliance**

- **HIPAA** **Certifications**

- **Data** retention **controls**

- **Customer** **data** **isolation** (in Premium and Dedicated tiers)

You should always:

- Inform users that AI is processing their data.

- Log interactions for auditability.

- Enable logging and metrics in Azure Monitor for anomaly tracking.

If using sensitive data, consider deploying services in containers within a secure VNet.

Combining Cognitive Services

Cognitive Services are modular by design. You can chain them together for more complex workflows.

Example: Voice-Activated Translator Bot

1. **Speech to Text** → Convert audio to text.

2. **Text Analytics** → Detect language.

3. **Translator** → Translate to user's preferred language.

4. **Text to Speech** → Deliver translated response as audio.

Each API is called sequentially or through Azure Functions for automation:

```
translated_text = translator.translate(input_text, to='fr')
spoken_output                                              =
speech_synthesizer.speak_text_async(translated_text).get()
```

Use Azure Logic Apps or Durable Functions to build scalable, stateful workflows.

Limitations and Considerations

While Cognitive Services are powerful, there are a few limitations:

- **Rate Limits**: APIs have request-per-second caps based on tier.

- **Customization**: Pre-trained models may not meet all domain-specific needs.

- **Latency**: Shared endpoints may introduce network latency; use regional endpoints.

- **Data Sovereignty**: Ensure the region aligns with legal/compliance requirements.

To overcome these, consider:

- Using **Custom Vision**, **Custom Speech**, or **LUIS** to train on your own data.

- Deploying services via **containers** for lower latency and data control.

- Upgrading to **enterprise pricing tiers** for higher throughput.

Summary

Azure Cognitive Services dramatically reduce the time, cost, and complexity of building intelligent applications. With powerful, scalable APIs covering vision, speech, language, decision-making, and search, they provide foundational capabilities that allow developers to inject AI into nearly any software solution.

Whether you're creating a customer support chatbot, a real-time translation app, or an AI-powered document processing pipeline, Cognitive Services will enable you to focus on your application's value rather than reinventing AI algorithms from scratch.

In the next sections, we'll dive into hands-on implementation, starting with Vision APIs—including Computer Vision and Face API—demonstrating how to analyze and interpret images with just a few lines of code.

Implementing Vision APIs (Computer Vision, Face API)

Computer vision is one of the most powerful and widely used domains in artificial intelligence. In Azure, the Vision APIs provide an intuitive and scalable way to analyze images and videos, detect and recognize faces, extract text, and build custom image classification models. This section will walk through the implementation of two of the most commonly used services in Azure Cognitive Services' Vision family: **Computer Vision API** and **Face API**.

These APIs allow developers to embed advanced image processing functionality into applications without requiring deep expertise in computer vision or deep learning. You will learn how to set up and authenticate Vision services, send requests to analyze content, and process the results for various practical use cases such as photo tagging, document digitization, and face detection.

Getting Started with Azure Vision Services

Before using the Vision APIs, you need to provision the relevant resources from the Azure Portal:

1. Navigate to the **Azure Portal**.

2. Click **Create a Resource > AI + Machine Learning > Computer Vision** or **Face**.

3. Choose a subscription, create or select a resource group, and set the region.

4. Once deployed, go to the resource and retrieve:

   o **Endpoint** (e.g., `https://<region>.api.cognitive.microsoft.com`)

   o **Key** (used to authenticate requests)

You can use the same credentials across multiple SDKs and REST APIs.

Overview of the Computer Vision API

The Computer Vision API provides capabilities for:

- **Image analysis**: Describe scenes, detect objects, and generate tags.

- **OCR (Optical Character Recognition)**: Extract printed or handwritten text.

- **Image categorization**: Identify themes like "outdoor", "food", or "text".

- **Thumbnail generation**: Crop and resize images based on content.

- **Spatial analysis**: Detect people and track movement in physical spaces.

Key Endpoints

- `analyze:` Analyze image content.
- `describe:` Generate natural language description.
- `read:` Perform OCR and extract text.
- `tag:` Generate keywords from image.
- `detectObjects:` Detect locations of objects.

Basic Image Analysis Example

REST API Call

```
POST
https://<region>.api.cognitive.microsoft.com/vision/v3.2/analyze?vis
ualFeatures=Description,Tags,Objects
Headers:
  Ocp-Apim-Subscription-Key: <your-api-key>
  Content-Type: application/json

Body:
{
  "url": "https://example.com/image.jpg"
}
```

Python SDK Example

```python
from        azure.cognitiveservices.vision.computervision        import
ComputerVisionClient
from msrest.authentication import CognitiveServicesCredentials

endpoint = "https://<region>.api.cognitive.microsoft.com"
key = "<your-key>"

client                =                ComputerVisionClient(endpoint,
CognitiveServicesCredentials(key))

url = "https://example.com/image.jpg"
result  =  client.analyze_image(url,  visual_features=["Description",
"Tags", "Objects"])
```

```
print("Description:", result.description.captions[0].text)
print("Tags:", [tag.name for tag in result.tags])
```

This code analyzes the image and outputs a caption and a list of identified tags and objects.

Optical Character Recognition (OCR)

Azure's OCR capabilities can extract text from photos of documents, menus, receipts, and handwritten notes. The read API is asynchronous and preferred over the legacy ocr endpoint.

Step-by-Step with Python

```
poller = client.read(url, raw=True)
operation_location = poller.headers["Operation-Location"]
operation_id = operation_location.split("/")[-1]

import time
while True:
    result = client.get_read_result(operation_id)
    if result.status.lower() not in ['notstarted', 'running']:
        break
    time.sleep(1)

if result.status == "succeeded":
    for page in result.analyze_result.read_results:
        for line in page.lines:
            print(line.text)
```

OCR is extremely useful for invoice processing, ID card scanning, and mobile form digitization.

Introduction to the Face API

The Face API detects and analyzes faces in images. Its capabilities include:

- **Face detection**: Locate faces and extract bounding boxes.

- **Facial attributes**: Age, emotion, gender, smile, head pose, facial hair, etc.

- **Face recognition:** Compare and identify individuals.

- **Face grouping:** Cluster similar faces.

Setting Up

Use the same approach as for Computer Vision: create the Face API resource in Azure Portal, retrieve your key and endpoint.

Detecting Faces in Images

REST Request

```
POST
https://<region>.api.cognitive.microsoft.com/face/v1.0/detect?return
FaceAttributes=age,gender,emotion
Headers:
  Ocp-Apim-Subscription-Key: <your-api-key>
  Content-Type: application/json

Body:
{
  "url": "https://example.com/portrait.jpg"
}
```

Python SDK Example

```python
from azure.cognitiveservices.vision.face import FaceClient
from msrest.authentication import CognitiveServicesCredentials

face_client = FaceClient(endpoint, CognitiveServicesCredentials(key))
img_url = "https://example.com/portrait.jpg"

faces = face_client.face.detect_with_url(
    img_url,
    return_face_attributes=["age", "gender", "emotion"]
)

for face in faces:
    print("Age:", face.face_attributes.age)
    print("Gender:", face.face_attributes.gender)
    print("Emotions:", face.face_attributes.emotion)
```

Face Verification and Grouping

Use Cases

- **Face verification**: Check if two images are of the same person.

- **Face identification**: Match a face against a database (Face List).

- **Face grouping**: Cluster unknown faces based on similarity.

Creating a Face List

```
face_client.face_list.create("friends",      name="Friends      List",
recognition_model="recognition_04")
face_client.face_list.add_face_from_url("friends",
"https://example.com/photo1.jpg")
face_client.face_list.add_face_from_url("friends",
"https://example.com/photo2.jpg")
```

Verifying Two Faces

```
verify_result    =    face_client.face.verify_face_to_face(face_id1,
face_id2)
print("Is same person:", verify_result.is_identical)
print("Confidence:", verify_result.confidence)
```

Real-World Applications

Use Case	Service	Description
ID card verification	Face + OCR	Extract text, detect and match photo to selfie
Retail analytics	Face + Vision	Count people, analyze demographics and sentiment
Document scanning	Vision (read)	Digitize paper forms and receipts
Visual content moderation	Vision + Moderator	Detect inappropriate or restricted visual content

Attendance tracking	Face API	Match faces from webcam feed to known identity list
Custom product tagging	Custom Vision	Train model to identify products in store or warehouse

Performance and Accuracy

- **Face API** supports multiple recognition models (`recognition_01`, `recognition_04`).

- **Detection Model 1** offers quick detection; Model 2 offers better accuracy.

- Use **recognition_04** for high-accuracy verification tasks.

- Accuracy may vary across demographic groups; test thoroughly before deploying at scale.

You can specify the model when calling the API:

```
face_client.face.detect_with_url(
    img_url,
    recognition_model='recognition_04',
    detection_model='detection_02'
)
```

Security, Privacy, and Compliance

Vision APIs process sensitive visual data, often including personally identifiable information (PII). Azure provides:

- **End-to-end encryption** for data in transit and at rest.

- **GDPR, HIPAA, and ISO** compliance.

- **Data residency controls** via regional deployment.

- **Access logging** and monitoring with Azure Monitor.

Important: Azure Cognitive Services do not retain images beyond processing time unless explicitly stored via user action (e.g., saving in a Face List).

Common Pitfalls and Best Practices

Pitfall	Recommendation
Sending large images	Resize or compress to reduce upload and processing time
Overuse of polling for OCR	Use exponential backoff and timeout checks
Poor face matching accuracy	Use high-resolution, front-facing, well-lit images
Storing API keys in code	Use Azure Key Vault + environment variables
Not using the right model	Specify correct `recognition_model` and `detection_model`
Assuming results are always accurate	Build fallback logic and allow for manual overrides

Summary

The Azure Computer Vision and Face APIs are production-ready, easy-to-integrate tools for infusing AI into your applications. From extracting text and analyzing visual scenes to identifying individuals and tracking facial expressions, these services can enhance the intelligence of any product—whether it's a mobile app, internal dashboard, surveillance system, or document management platform.

By following the practices and examples in this section, you can quickly get started with visual AI in Azure, scale to complex use cases, and build secure, performant, and user-friendly intelligent solutions.

In the next section, we'll dive into language-focused capabilities using Language Understanding (LUIS) and Azure Translator to power intelligent conversations and cross-lingual apps.

Language Understanding and Translation (LUIS, Translator)

Natural Language Processing (NLP) enables applications to understand, interpret, and generate human language. In Azure, two flagship services empower developers to create intelligent, language-aware applications: **Language Understanding (LUIS)** and **Azure**

Translator. Together, they allow software to extract meaning from text or speech, identify user intent, translate between languages, and support multilingual, conversational interfaces.

This section provides a comprehensive guide to implementing LUIS and Translator into your applications. You'll learn how to build, train, and publish language models, integrate them with APIs, handle translations in real-time, and apply these tools in real-world scenarios like customer support bots, virtual assistants, global e-commerce platforms, and more.

What Is LUIS?

Language Understanding (LUIS) is a cloud-based conversational AI service that enables developers to build natural language into apps, bots, and IoT devices. Unlike basic keyword-based approaches, LUIS applies machine learning to understand user intent and extract key information (entities) from utterances.

Core Concepts

- **Utterances**: Example phrases users might say.

- **Intents**: The action or goal behind a user's input (e.g., BookFlight, CheckWeather).

- **Entities**: Specific details extracted from the utterance (e.g., location, date, person).

- **Prebuilt Domains**: Ready-to-use models for common scenarios like calendar, alarm, weather.

- **Custom Entities**: User-defined information you want to extract (e.g., product names).

Creating a LUIS App

1. Visit https://www.luis.ai and sign in with your Azure account.

2. Create a new LUIS application, name it (e.g., TravelAgentAI), and choose a culture (e.g., English).

3. Add **intents** such as:

   o BookFlight

   o CancelBooking

   o GetWeather

4. Add **utterances** to each intent:
   - "I want to book a flight to London next Friday."
   - "Cancel my reservation to Paris."

5. Create **entities** like:
   - Location
   - Date
   - FlightClass

Use built-in entity types or define patterns with regular expressions or machine-learned extraction.

Training and Publishing

Once your intents and entities are configured:

- Click **Train** to train the model with your current utterances.
- Click **Test** to validate predictions in real time.
- Click **Publish** to make your model accessible via API.

LUIS will provide an endpoint URL and a prediction key for calling the model.

```
POST
https://<region>.api.cognitive.microsoft.com/luis/prediction/v3.0/ap
ps/<app-id>/slots/production/predict?subscription-
key=<key>&query=Book+me+a+flight+to+Rome
```

The response includes the top intent, confidence score, and extracted entities.

Calling LUIS from a Python App

```python
import requests
```

```
url                                                                    =
"https://<region>.api.cognitive.microsoft.com/luis/prediction/v3.0/a
pps/<app-id>/slots/production/predict"
params = {
    "subscription-key": "<your-key>",
    "query": "Book me a flight to New York next Thursday"
}
response = requests.get(url, params=params)
data = response.json()

intent = data["prediction"]["topIntent"]
entities = data["prediction"]["entities"]

print("Intent:", intent)
print("Entities:", entities)
```

LUIS helps applications interpret natural input and take the appropriate action, making it ideal for chatbots, form auto-fill, and intelligent routing.

Introduction to Azure Translator

Azure Translator is a fully managed, real-time, AI-powered service that provides neural machine translation across 90+ languages. It can translate raw text, documents, and even spoken content.

Translator is REST-based and integrates with Azure Speech for speech-to-speech and speech-to-text translation.

Use Cases

- Real-time translation in messaging apps.

- Multilingual product catalogs and e-commerce.

- Localization of content and documentation.

- Language support in global chatbots.

- Mobile travel assistant apps.

Basic Text Translation

To start using Translator:

1. Go to the **Azure Portal**.

2. Create a **Translator** resource under **AI + Machine Learning**.

3. Retrieve the **endpoint** and **key**.

Sample REST Call

```
POST      https://api.cognitive.microsofttranslator.com/translate?api-
version=3.0&to=fr
Headers:
  Ocp-Apim-Subscription-Key: <your-key>
  Content-Type: application/json

Body:
[
  { "Text": "Hello, how can I help you?" }
]
```

Python Example

```
import requests, uuid, json

endpoint = "https://api.cognitive.microsofttranslator.com"
path = "/translate?api-version=3.0"
params = "&to=es"
constructed_url = endpoint + path + params

headers = {
    'Ocp-Apim-Subscription-Key': '<your-key>',
    'Content-Type': 'application/json',
    'X-ClientTraceId': str(uuid.uuid4())
}

body = [{ 'text': 'I need help with my order.' }]
response = requests.post(constructed_url, headers=headers, json=body)
result = response.json()

print("Translated Text:", result[0]['translations'][0]['text'])
```

Auto-Detect Source Language

You don't need to specify the source language—Translator can auto-detect it.

```
POST      https://api.cognitive.microsofttranslator.com/translate?api-
version=3.0&to=de
Body:
[
  { "Text": "Bonjour tout le monde" }
]
```

Response:

```
{
  "detectedLanguage": {
    "language": "fr",
    "score": 1.0
  },
  "translations": [
    { "text": "Hallo zusammen", "to": "de" }
  ]
}
```

Document and Batch Translation

You can upload files (Word, PDF, Excel) and translate them in batches using Azure Blob Storage:

1. Create a **document translation job**.

2. Point to source and destination containers.

3. Use the REST API or Azure SDK to initiate and track jobs.

```
az cognitiveservices account identity assign --name TranslatorService
--resource-group ai-rg
```

Real-Time Speech Translation

By combining Translator with **Azure Speech Services**, you can translate spoken audio in real-time:

- Convert speech to text using **Speech-to-Text**.

- Translate the text using Translator API.

- Convert back to audio using **Text-to-Speech**.

This enables:

- Cross-language meetings and conferences.

- Interactive voice-enabled assistants.

- Real-time translation earbuds and devices.

Azure offers an SDK for integrated speech translation:

```python
import azure.cognitiveservices.speech as speechsdk

speech_config = speechsdk.SpeechConfig(subscription="<key>", region="<region>")
speech_config.speech_recognition_language = "en-US"
speech_config.add_target_language("ja")
speech_config.add_target_language("fr")

translation_recognizer = speechsdk.translation.TranslationRecognizer(speech_config=speech_config)

result = translation_recognizer.recognize_once()
print("Recognized:", result.text)
print("Translations:", result.translations)
```

Combining LUIS and Translator

You can chain Translator and LUIS to build multilingual chatbots:

1. Detect user input language and translate to English.

2. Send translated input to LUIS for intent recognition.

3. Generate a response based on detected intent.

4. Translate the response back to the original language.

This allows you to maintain a single LUIS model while serving users in any supported language.

Real-World Use Cases

Application	Tools Used	Description
Customer Support Bot	LUIS + Translator + QnA Maker	Understand customer queries, respond in their language
International Booking System	Translator + LUIS	Accept and interpret requests in native language
Travel Assistant	Translator + Speech Services	Translate spoken input and provide voice response
E-Commerce Product Description Sync	Translator + Azure Logic Apps	Translate catalog data for multiple regions
Smart Healthcare Intake Forms	LUIS + Translator	Detect intent from symptoms across languages

Best Practices

- Train LUIS with diverse, domain-specific utterances.

- Continuously review user input logs to identify and correct misclassifications.

- Use content filters in Translator for sensitive content.

- Deploy LUIS and Translator in the same Azure region to reduce latency.

- Implement language fallback logic for unsupported languages.

Limitations and Considerations

- LUIS supports a limited number of languages compared to Translator.

- Translator provides real-time translation but may not capture nuance in technical domains.

- For secure applications, route Translator and LUIS through **Azure Private Link** or deploy container versions.

- Monitor costs if using services at high volume—use batch processing where possible.

Summary

Together, Azure LUIS and Translator unlock the ability to understand and respond to users in any language with natural and intelligent interactions. From real-time conversations to processing user queries across borders, these services bridge the gap between human language and machine logic.

By combining natural language understanding with translation, you can build inclusive, multilingual, and highly responsive applications that feel intuitive no matter where your users are or what language they speak.

Next, we'll explore Azure's speech services, covering how to recognize, transcribe, and synthesize voice data to complete the foundation of a conversational AI system.

Speech Recognition and Synthesis

Speech is one of the most natural forms of human communication. Azure's Speech service enables developers to build applications that can listen, understand, and speak with users. From transcribing meetings to creating digital voice assistants and accessibility tools, speech recognition and synthesis (Text-to-Speech) form a core part of Azure Cognitive Services' offering.

This section explores how to use Azure's Speech services to convert spoken audio to text, generate human-like speech from text, perform speaker verification, and even translate speech in real-time. We'll cover practical use cases, implementation guides, and best practices to help you build robust, scalable, and multilingual voice-driven applications.

Introduction to Azure Speech Services

Azure's Speech service is a unified offering for all things voice:

- **Speech-to-Text** (STT): Transcribes spoken audio into written text.

- **Text-to-Speech** (TTS): Synthesizes spoken audio from written text.

- **Speech Translation**: Translates spoken language into another language.

- **Speaker Recognition**: Verifies and identifies users based on voice signatures.

- **Custom Voice**: Allows creation of custom voice fonts using your own data.

These services can be consumed via SDKs, REST APIs, containers, or integrated into Azure Bot Service and Logic Apps.

Setting Up the Speech Resource

To get started:

1. Go to the Azure Portal.

2. Navigate to **Create a Resource** > **AI + Machine Learning** > **Speech**.

3. Choose your subscription, region, and pricing tier.

4. After creation, go to the resource overview and copy the **Key** and **Endpoint**.

Azure recommends using the **East US**, **West Europe**, or **Southeast Asia** regions for optimal performance.

Install the Azure Speech SDK:

```
pip install azure-cognitiveservices-speech
```

Speech-to-Text (Transcription)

Azure's Speech-to-Text converts spoken language into readable text, enabling applications like voice commands, transcription, and meeting notes generation.

Basic Transcription in Python

```
import azure.cognitiveservices.speech as speechsdk

speech_config = speechsdk.SpeechConfig(subscription="YOUR_KEY",
region="YOUR_REGION")
```

```
audio_config = speechsdk.audio.AudioConfig(filename="audio.wav")

speech_recognizer                                                  =
speechsdk.SpeechRecognizer(speech_config=speech_config,
audio_config=audio_config)
result = speech_recognizer.recognize_once()

print("Recognized:", result.text)
```

You can also transcribe audio from a microphone:

```
audio_config = speechsdk.AudioConfig(use_default_microphone=True)
```

Continuous and Real-Time Recognition

Use the `start_continuous_recognition()` method for real-time transcription:

```
def handle_result(evt):
    print("Recognized:", evt.result.text)

speech_recognizer.recognized.connect(handle_result)
speech_recognizer.start_continuous_recognition()

import time
time.sleep(10)
speech_recognizer.stop_continuous_recognition()
```

This is useful for meeting transcription, streaming subtitles, or dictation tools.

Enhancing Accuracy

- **Language Models**: Use a custom language model for domain-specific vocabulary.

- **Punctuation and Formatting**: Automatically formats output using AI-based punctuation.

- **Noise Suppression**: Optimized for real-world environments.

To enable enhanced models:

```
speech_config.speech_recognition_language = "en-US"
speech_config.enable_dictation()
```

Custom Speech

Azure allows you to build **Custom Speech Models** by uploading domain-specific recordings and transcripts to the Custom Speech portal at https://speech.azure.com. This improves recognition for specialized jargon, accents, or low-quality audio.

Text-to-Speech (Synthesis)

Text-to-Speech (TTS) converts written text into natural-sounding audio. Azure provides over 400 voices across 140+ languages and variants, with options for standard and neural voices.

Basic Synthesis in Python

```
speech_config     =     speechsdk.SpeechConfig(subscription="YOUR_KEY",
region="YOUR_REGION")
synthesizer                                                          =
speechsdk.SpeechSynthesizer(speech_config=speech_config)

text = "Hello, welcome to Azure Speech Services!"
result = synthesizer.speak_text_async(text).get()
```

You can also save the output to a file:

```
audio_config                                                         =
speechsdk.audio.AudioOutputConfig(filename="output.wav")
synthesizer                                                          =
speechsdk.SpeechSynthesizer(speech_config=speech_config,
audio_config=audio_config)
```

Customizing the Voice Output

Azure supports **SSML** (Speech Synthesis Markup Language) to customize speech pitch, rate, volume, and emphasis.

```
<speak version='1.0' xml:lang='en-US'>
  <voice name='en-US-JennyNeural'>
```

```
    <prosody rate='slow' pitch='+5%'>Your balance is now five hundred
dollars.</prosody>
  </voice>
</speak>
```

Use `speak_ssml_async()` to synthesize SSML-defined speech.

```
ssml_string = """<speak version='1.0' xml:lang='en-US'>
<voice name='en-US-AriaNeural'>
<prosody rate='-10.00%' pitch='+5.00%'>Good morning! Your appointment
is at 10:30 AM.</prosody>
</voice></speak>"""

synthesizer.speak_ssml_async(ssml_string).get()
```

Speech Translation

Translate spoken audio from one language into another, in real-time.

```
speech_config = speechsdk.translation.SpeechTranslationConfig(
    subscription="YOUR_KEY",
    region="YOUR_REGION"
)
speech_config.speech_recognition_language = "en-US"
speech_config.add_target_language("fr")

recognizer                                                        =
speechsdk.translation.TranslationRecognizer(speech_config=speech_con
fig)

result = recognizer.recognize_once()
print("Source:", result.text)
print("French Translation:", result.translations["fr"])
```

This is ideal for language learning apps, travel assistants, and international customer service.

Speaker Recognition

Azure supports:

- **Speaker Verification**: Confirm if a person matches a voice print.

- **Speaker Identification**: Identify which enrolled speaker spoke.

To use this:

1. Use the **Speaker Recognition API** (not included in Speech SDK).

2. Enroll speaker voice samples.

3. Call verify or identify endpoints with new samples.

This is useful for secure login systems, personalized assistants, and forensic analysis.

Real-World Use Cases

Use Case	Feature	Description
Transcribing calls	Speech-to-Text	Real-time or recorded audio transcription
Accessibility tools	Text-to-Speech	Convert digital content to audio for visually impaired
Voice assistants	STT + TTS + LUIS	Full conversation loop powered by natural voice
Language learning apps	Speech Translation	Listen and translate speech between languages
Secure voice login	Speaker Recognition	Authenticate users by voice
Voice-controlled dashboards	STT + Commands	Hands-free navigation and commands

Handling Audio Formats and Devices

Azure supports multiple input formats:

- WAV (PCM or MP3)

- MP3

- Microphone stream (live input)

You can adjust the audio input source using:

```
audio_config = speechsdk.AudioConfig(filename="interview.mp3")
```

And for microphone input:

```
audio_config = speechsdk.AudioConfig(use_default_microphone=True)
```

Monitoring, Logs, and Performance

Enable logging with:

```
speech_config.enable_audio_logging()
```

Use **Azure Monitor** to track usage, error rates, and performance metrics. Set up alerts for:

- High error rates

- Excessive latency

- Cost thresholds

Use diagnostic logs to analyze accuracy and response times across languages and accents.

Best Practices

- Use **neural voices** for improved realism and user engagement.

- Cache speech synthesis responses to reduce repeat calls and cost.

- Train **Custom Speech Models** for domain-specific jargon.

- Use **SSML** to create expressive speech experiences.

- Optimize microphone input by reducing background noise and using directional mics.

- Use **Auto Language Detection** to simplify multilingual input handling.

Limitations and Considerations

- Free tier includes limited minutes per month—monitor quotas.

- Real-time translation supports fewer languages than Text Translation.

- Custom voice training requires licensed audio data and ethical compliance.

- Speaker Recognition is only available in selected regions.

Always verify **data privacy requirements**, especially when processing biometric voice data. Consider deploying Speech containers in secured environments for offline or private processing.

Summary

Azure's Speech service provides a comprehensive set of tools for enabling voice-driven intelligence in your applications. From accurate transcription and lifelike voice synthesis to speaker verification and real-time translation, Speech services can serve as the auditory interface for your users—helping your apps feel more natural, inclusive, and responsive.

Whether you're building an accessible reader, an intelligent meeting assistant, or a multilingual chatbot, Azure Speech gives you the power to turn sound into structured intelligence—and back again.

In the next section, we'll explore how to enhance your applications further by integrating intelligent search capabilities using Azure Search and related services.

Integrating Search Capabilities with Azure Search

Search is a fundamental capability of intelligent applications. Whether you're enabling users to explore a product catalog, query a document archive, or discover entities within a knowledge base, fast and relevant search results enhance usability and engagement. Azure AI-powered search capabilities—particularly through **Azure AI Search** (formerly Azure Cognitive Search)—combine traditional indexing with artificial intelligence to deliver meaningful, filtered, and context-aware search experiences.

This section explores how to integrate search functionality into your applications using Azure AI Search. It includes end-to-end guidance on setting up search indexes, ingesting content, applying cognitive skills for enrichment, and implementing intelligent features like autocomplete, synonyms, filtering, faceting, and semantic search.

Overview of Azure AI Search

Azure AI Search is a fully managed search-as-a-service platform that allows developers to build sophisticated search experiences over private, structured or unstructured content. It is designed to be scalable, secure, and extensible with built-in AI enrichment capabilities.

Key features include:

- Full-text search with ranked relevance

- Natural language search with semantic ranking

- AI enrichment (OCR, language detection, entity recognition)

- Faceting, filtering, and scoring profiles

- REST APIs and SDKs for integration

- Cognitive Skills pipeline for advanced scenarios

- Multi-language support

Azure Search supports both structured and unstructured content types, including PDFs, DOCX files, JSON, SQL data, Azure Blob Storage content, and more.

Creating an Azure Search Service

1. Go to the Azure Portal.

2. Click **Create a resource** > **Web** > **Azure AI Search**.

3. Choose your subscription and region.

4. Choose a pricing tier (Free tier is available for testing).

5. Click **Review + Create**, then **Create**.

After deployment, access your service and obtain:

- **Service**   **name**

- **Admin**   **API**   **Key**

- **Query**   **API**   **Key**

- **Endpoint   URL**   (e.g.,   `https://<your-service>.search.windows.net`)

Defining a Search Index

An **index** in Azure Search is similar to a database schema—it defines the fields and types of content that can be searched.

Sample Index Definition

```
{
  "name": "documents-index",
  "fields": [
    { "name": "id", "type": "Edm.String", "key": true },
    { "name": "title", "type": "Edm.String", "searchable": true },
    { "name": "content", "type": "Edm.String", "searchable": true },
    { "name": "category", "type": "Edm.String", "filterable": true,
"facetable": true },
    { "name": "tags", "type": "Collection(Edm.String)", "searchable":
true, "facetable": true }
  ]
}
```

To create the index, make a REST request:

```
PUT      https://<your-service>.search.windows.net/indexes/documents-
index?api-version=2021-04-30-Preview
Headers:
  Content-Type: application/json
  api-key: <admin-key>
Body: (index definition above)
```

Alternatively, use the Azure SDK for Python:

```
from azure.search.documents.indexes import SearchIndexClient
from azure.core.credentials import AzureKeyCredential
```

```
endpoint = "https://<your-service>.search.windows.net"
key = "<your-admin-key>"

index_client = SearchIndexClient(endpoint, AzureKeyCredential(key))
index_client.create_index(index_definition)
```

Ingesting and Indexing Data

Data can be ingested manually, via APIs, or through **indexers** that automatically pull content from Azure Blob Storage, Cosmos DB, or SQL.

Example: Upload Documents via REST API

```
POST     https://<your-service>.search.windows.net/indexes/documents-
index/docs/index?api-version=2021-04-30-Preview
Headers:
  Content-Type: application/json
  api-key: <admin-key>
Body:
{
  "value": [
    {
      "@search.action": "upload",
      "id": "1",
      "title": "Azure AI Overview",
      "content": "Azure AI provides cognitive and machine learning
services...",
      "category": "Documentation",
      "tags": ["azure", "ai", "cloud"]
    }
  ]
}
```

You can also batch upload multiple documents using the SDK:

```
from azure.search.documents import SearchClient

search_client    =    SearchClient(endpoint,    "documents-index",
AzureKeyCredential(key))
```

```
documents = [
    {
        "id": "2",
        "title": "Building with Azure Search",
        "content": "Learn    how    to    build    intelligent    search
solutions...",
        "category": "Tutorial",
        "tags": ["azure", "search", "tutorial"]
    }
]


search_client.upload_documents(documents)
```

Enriching Content with Cognitive Skills

Azure AI Search supports **skillsets**, which apply cognitive services during indexing to extract insights from raw content.

Available built-in skills include:

- **OCR (Computer Vision)** for extracting text from images and PDFs

- **Entity Recognition** (e.g., people, locations, organizations)

- **Language   Detection**

- **Sentiment   Analysis**

- **Text   Translation**

These enrichments are configured in a **skillset**, which is linked to an indexer.

Sample Skillset (JSON)

```
{
  "name": "document-skillset",
  "skills": [
    {
      "@odata.type":
"#Microsoft.Skills.Text.EntityRecognitionSkill",
      "categories": ["organization", "location", "person"],
      "inputs": [
        { "name": "text", "source": "/document/content" }
```

```
    ],
    "outputs": [
      { "name": "organizations", "targetName": "orgs" }
    ]
  }
 ]
}
```

Building the Search Experience

Once the index is built and populated, users can query it using the search endpoint:

```
GET       https://<your-service>.search.windows.net/indexes/documents-
index/docs?api-version=2021-04-30-Preview&search=azure
Headers:
  api-key: <query-key>
```

Features You Can Enable

- **Faceting**: Show result breakdowns (e.g., count by category)

- **Filtering**: Narrow results by field values

- **Autocomplete**: Suggest queries as the user types

- **Synonyms**: Map related terms (e.g., "AI" and "Artificial Intelligence")

- **Highlighting**: Highlight matched terms in snippets

Example with filters and facets:

```
GET   /indexes/documents-index/docs?search=cloud&$filter=category   eq
'Tutorial'&facet=tags
```

Semantic Search (Preview)

Semantic Search enhances traditional keyword-based search by applying AI models to improve understanding of the query's meaning.

Capabilities include:

- Contextual ranking using deep learning

- Captions and highlights

- Better support for conversational queries

To enable, switch the query type:

```
GET             /indexes/documents-index/docs?api-version=2021-04-30-
Preview&search=azure&queryType=semantic&semanticConfiguration=defaul
t
```

Semantic Search requires a Standard tier or above and uses pre-trained models developed by Microsoft Research.

UI Integration

Azure Search integrates easily with front-end frameworks:

- JavaScript + REST for SPAs

- Blazor, React, or Angular apps using SDKs

- Azure Bot Framework for conversational search

- Microsoft Power Apps for low-code experiences

You can embed search in a webpage using React:

```
fetch("https://<service>.search.windows.net/indexes/documents-
index/docs?api-version=2021-04-30-Preview&search=azure", {
  headers: { "api-key": "<query-key>" }
})
.then(response => response.json())
.then(data => console.log(data.value));
```

For complex enterprise apps, use Azure Cognitive Search SDKs and implement dynamic filtering, autocomplete, result scoring, and paging.

Real-World Use Cases

Application	Description
Knowledge Base Search	Index technical documents, extract entities, provide smart answers
E-Commerce Product Discovery	Enable filters, facets, synonyms, and product ranking
Intranet Content Search	Build employee portals with department, role, and tag filtering
Media Archives	OCR and transcribe video/audio content for searchable access
Legal Document Analysis	Index PDFs, detect named entities, and classify contract types
Academic Research Discovery	Index research papers and categorize by topic, author, institution

Best Practices

- **Design index carefully**: Avoid unnecessary fields; optimize for relevance and storage.

- **Use cognitive enrichment selectively**: It can be costly—apply only where needed.

- **Apply scoring profiles**: Prioritize results based on importance (e.g., recency, ratings).

- **Secure access**: Use query keys for client-side apps, admin keys for server-side operations.

- **Monitor search logs**: Analyze popular queries, no-results queries, and improve relevance.

Cost Considerations

Azure AI Search pricing depends on:

- **Replica** and **partition** counts

- **Search** **units** **(scaling)**

- **Cognitive** **Skill** **executions**

- **Storage** **and** **indexing** **size**

Free tier allows:

- 3 indexes

- 50 MB storage

- Limited throughput

Production scenarios should estimate based on document size, query volume, and enrichment needs using the Azure Pricing Calculator.

Summary

Azure AI Search enables developers to build rich, intelligent, and fast search experiences across a variety of domains. By combining search indexing with machine learning-powered enrichment and relevance tuning, you can turn unstructured data into usable knowledge that users can find, filter, and explore effortlessly.

From knowledge bases and document repositories to dynamic product catalogs and content portals, Azure Search serves as a vital component in AI-driven applications—enhancing discovery, comprehension, and decision-making.

In the next chapter, we'll shift from pre-trained Cognitive Services to custom model development using Azure Machine Learning Studio, where you'll build, train, and deploy machine learning models tailored to your specific business needs.

Chapter 4: Building Intelligent Apps with Azure Machine Learning

Introduction to Azure Machine Learning Studio

Azure Machine Learning (Azure ML) is a robust, end-to-end platform for building, training, and deploying machine learning models at scale. It is designed for data scientists, ML engineers, and AI developers who need to develop and operationalize AI solutions quickly and efficiently using Azure's secure and scalable cloud infrastructure.

Azure Machine Learning Studio, a core component of Azure ML, provides both a code-first environment (for Python/R developers) and a low-code/no-code environment (for citizen data scientists) to manage every aspect of the ML lifecycle—from data preparation and experimentation to model training, evaluation, deployment, and monitoring.

This section will guide you through the key features, architecture, and workflows within Azure ML Studio, showing how to start using this powerful platform to create intelligent applications that learn from data and evolve over time.

Why Use Azure Machine Learning?

Azure ML is designed for enterprise-grade machine learning projects that demand scalability, security, and reproducibility. Its primary benefits include:

- **Unified environment** for data prep, training, deployment, and monitoring.

- **Low-code and code-first options** with Jupyter notebooks, Visual Studio Code integration, and a drag-and-drop Designer.

- **MLOps capabilities** for CI/CD, model versioning, and lifecycle automation.

- **Scalable compute** options including CPU, GPU, and FPGA clusters.

- **Integration** with Azure Data Factory, DevOps, Blob Storage, Databricks, and Power BI.

- **Enterprise governance** including RBAC, audit logs, encryption, and compliance support.

Azure ML supports both classical ML and deep learning frameworks like TensorFlow, PyTorch, Scikit-learn, XGBoost, and ONNX.

Getting Started with Azure ML Studio

1. **Log into the Azure Portal.**

2. **Navigate to "Machine Learning"** in the service menu.

3. **Create a new ML workspace:**

   - Resource Group: `ml-rg`

   - Workspace Name: `ml-workspace`

   - Region: Choose the one closest to your users or data.

4. Once deployed, go to **studio.azureml.net** or click "Launch Studio" from the workspace overview.

Azure ML Studio Interface Overview

The ML Studio interface consists of:

- **Home/Dashboard**: Access to recent activities and tutorials.

- **Notebooks**: Jupyter environment for code-first development.

- **Designer**: Low-code drag-and-drop canvas for building ML pipelines visually.

- **Automated ML**: Configure experiments that automatically search for the best model.

- **Datasets**: Register and manage tabular or file datasets.

- **Experiments**: View run history and logs.

- **Pipelines**: Define reusable ML workflows.

- **Models**: Register and version trained models.

- **Endpoints**: Manage deployed models with REST APIs.

- **Compute**: Create and manage training and inference clusters.

Each component helps simplify the end-to-end lifecycle of AI development.

ML Development Options

Azure ML supports different user personas:

Code-First (Python/R)

- Use Jupyter notebooks within Studio or locally via VS Code.
- Use AzureML SDK (`azureml-core`) to access all workspace assets.
- Recommended for experienced developers and data scientists.

Low-Code (Designer)

- Drag-and-drop modules to build pipelines visually.
- Ideal for quick prototyping or non-coders.
- Supports built-in ML algorithms and preprocessing steps.

Automated ML (AutoML)

- Automatically train, tune, and compare multiple models.
- Select best model based on metric (e.g., AUC, accuracy, RMSE).
- Supports classification, regression, and time-series forecasting.

AzureML SDK Essentials

Install AzureML SDK:

```
pip install azureml-core azureml-dataset azureml-train-core
```

Sample setup in Python:

```python
from azureml.core import Workspace

ws = Workspace.from_config()
print("Workspace name:", ws.name)
```

You can also create the workspace programmatically:

```
from azureml.core import Workspace

ws = Workspace.create(
    name='ml-workspace',
    subscription_id='your-subscription-id',
    resource_group='ml-rg',
    location='eastus'
)
```

Creating a Compute Instance

To run notebooks or train models interactively, create a compute instance:

1. Go to **Compute** > **Compute Instances** > **New**.

2. Choose a VM type (e.g., Standard_DS3_v2 for CPU or Standard_NC6 for GPU).

3. Assign a name and start the instance.

Compute instances are pre-configured with Python, Jupyter, and popular ML libraries.

Registering and Exploring Datasets

Azure ML supports two dataset types:

- **Tabular Dataset**: Structured tables, e.g., CSV files.

- **File Dataset**: Unstructured data like images, audio, or PDFs.

Upload via the UI or SDK:

```
from azureml.core import Dataset

datastore = ws.get_default_datastore()
dataset = Dataset.Tabular.from_delimited_files(path=(datastore,
'data/iris.csv'))

dataset = dataset.register(workspace=ws, name='iris-dataset',
create_new_version=True)
```

Preview and visualize datasets in Studio for initial inspection.

Using Designer to Build a Model Pipeline

1. Go to **Designer** and click **New** **Pipeline**.
2. Drag the following modules:

   ○ **Dataset**: e.g., "Iris dataset"

   ○ **Split** **Data**

   ○ **Train** **Model**

   ○ **Score** **Model**

   ○ **Evaluate** **Model**

3. Choose the algorithm (e.g., Decision Tree Classifier).
4. Connect modules and run the pipeline.

Once run is complete, explore results, register the model, and deploy it via endpoints.

Automated ML Workflow

1. Select a dataset.
2. Choose the prediction target (label).
3. Define the ML task (e.g., classification).
4. Configure compute and training time.
5. Let AutoML run and compare dozens of algorithms.

You'll get:

● Best model with explanation

● Feature importance scores

- Registered   model   artifact

This is ideal for domain experts or business analysts with limited coding skills.

ML Pipelines and Reusability

Azure ML Pipelines allow you to define multi-step workflows using Python:

```python
from azureml.pipeline.steps import PythonScriptStep
from azureml.pipeline.core import Pipeline

step = PythonScriptStep(
    name='Train Model',
    script_name='train.py',
    compute_target=compute_target,
    source_directory='scripts'
)

pipeline = Pipeline(workspace=ws, steps=[step])
pipeline.validate()
pipeline.run()
```

Pipelines support:

- Data   preprocessing

- Feature   engineering

- Model   training

- Model   evaluation

- Parallelization

These can be triggered from CI/CD tools like GitHub Actions or Azure DevOps.

Managing Experiments and Runs

Every time you train a model, an **Experiment Run** is logged.

You can view:

- Logs (stdout/stderr)

- Metrics (accuracy, loss, AUC)

- Model files

- Plots (matplotlib, seaborn)

Python example:

```python
from azureml.core import Experiment

experiment = Experiment(workspace=ws, name='iris-training')
run = experiment.start_logging()

# Training code here
run.log("accuracy", 0.93)
run.complete()
```

Runs can be compared, tagged, and reused to reproduce results.

Registering and Deploying Models

Once trained, models are versioned and stored in the **Model Registry**.

```python
from azureml.core.model import Model

model = Model.register(workspace=ws,
                       model_path='outputs/model.pkl',
                       model_name='iris-classifier')
```

Deploy to an endpoint:

```python
from azureml.core.webservice import AciWebservice
from azureml.core.model import InferenceConfig

inference_config = InferenceConfig(entry_script="score.py",
environment=myenv)
```

```
deployment_config = AciWebservice.deploy_configuration(cpu_cores=1,
memory_gb=1)

service = Model.deploy(workspace=ws,
                       name="iris-endpoint",
                       models=[model],
                       inference_config=inference_config,
                       deployment_config=deployment_config)

service.wait_for_deployment(show_output=True)
print(service.scoring_uri)
```

Summary

Azure Machine Learning Studio provides a complete environment for the modern AI lifecycle. Whether you are a seasoned data scientist looking for deep customization or a domain expert using low-code tools, Azure ML meets your needs.

Its flexibility across environments—Designer, AutoML, Notebooks—combined with powerful features like model tracking, explainability, pipelines, and enterprise security, makes it a top choice for building intelligent applications.

As we proceed to the next sections, you'll learn how to prepare data effectively, run scalable experiments, and optimize your models using Azure ML's advanced capabilities.

Data Preparation and Experimentation

Data is the foundation of every machine learning project. No matter how sophisticated your model or algorithms, the quality, relevance, and preparation of your data will directly impact your outcomes. In Azure Machine Learning, data preparation is tightly integrated into the platform through built-in tools, notebooks, datasets, data labeling projects, and support for scalable data processing pipelines.

This section explores the full lifecycle of data preparation and experimentation in Azure ML: from ingestion and cleansing to transformation and feature engineering. It covers best practices, automation techniques, and tooling available for preparing your data efficiently and reproducibly—whether you're working with CSV files, images, databases, or big data stored in Azure Blob Storage or Data Lake.

Ingesting and Registering Data

Azure Machine Learning offers several ways to load and register your data:

1. **Direct Uploads**: Upload small files from local disk through the Azure ML Studio UI.

2. **Datastores**: Reference external storage like Azure Blob, Azure Files, or Azure Data Lake.

3. **Datasets**: Logical containers for versioned data, used in experiments and pipelines.

Creating a Datastore

Datastores abstract connection to data storage:

```
from azureml.core import Workspace, Datastore

ws = Workspace.from_config()
datastore = Datastore.register_azure_blob_container(
    workspace=ws,
    datastore_name='data_blob',
    container_name='ml-data',
    account_name='yourstorageaccount',
    account_key='yourkey'
)
```

Creating a Dataset

```
from azureml.core import Dataset

dataset    =    Dataset.Tabular.from_delimited_files(path=(datastore,
'iris/iris.csv'))
dataset = dataset.register(workspace=ws,
                           name='iris-dataset',
                           create_new_version=True)
```

You can now use this dataset across notebooks, pipelines, and AutoML experiments.

Exploring and Profiling Data

Understanding your data's shape, distribution, and quality is critical. Azure ML provides tools to help inspect and profile datasets:

Data Exploration in Notebooks

```
df = dataset.to_pandas_dataframe()
print(df.head())
```

```
print(df.describe())
```

Data Profiling in Azure Studio

- Select a dataset from the **Datasets** tab.
- Click **Profile** to generate visual stats like:
  - Null value percentage
  - Cardinality
  - Mean, min, max
  - Histogram distribution

This helps you identify outliers, missing data, and skew.

Cleaning and Preprocessing

Common cleaning steps include:

- Removing duplicates
- Handling missing values
- Encoding categorical features
- Normalizing or scaling features

```
df.dropna(inplace=True)
df['species'] = df['species'].astype('category').cat.codes
```

Use Scikit-learn pipelines for reusable transformations:

```
from sklearn.preprocessing import StandardScaler
from sklearn.pipeline import Pipeline

pipeline = Pipeline([
    ('scaler', StandardScaler())
])
```

```
X_scaled = pipeline.fit_transform(df.drop(columns=['species']))
```

You can persist transformation logic using `joblib`:

```
import joblib
joblib.dump(pipeline, 'preprocess.joblib')
```

Feature Engineering

Feature engineering transforms raw inputs into useful signals for model learning. This may include:

- Creating derived columns (e.g., `bmi = weight / height^2`)

- Binning   continuous   features

- Extracting   time-based   features   (day   of   week,   hour)

- Encoding   text   using   TF-IDF,   word   embeddings,   or   tokenization

- Image   augmentation   or   resizing

```
df['bmi'] = df['weight_kg'] / (df['height_m'] ** 2)
df['hour'] = pd.to_datetime(df['timestamp']).dt.hour
```

Leverage libraries like:

- Pandas,   NumPy   (tabular)

- OpenCV,   PIL,   torchvision   (images)

- spaCy,   NLTK,   HuggingFace   (text)

Data Labeling Projects

For supervised learning, labeled data is essential. Azure ML provides a **Data Labeling** service for:

- Image   classification

- Object   detection

- Text   classification

- Named   entity   recognition   (NER)

Steps to launch a labeling project:

1. Upload   raw   data   into   Azure   Blob   Storage.

2. Go   to   **Data   Labeling**   in   Azure   ML   Studio.

3. Choose   the   labeling   task   and   connect   the   dataset.

4. Define   labels   and   assign   tasks   to   human   labelers.

5. Monitor   progress   and   export   the   labeled   dataset.

Labeled data can be exported as a new dataset version or JSON-compatible format.

Partitioning Data

Split data into training, validation, and test sets for proper model evaluation:

```
from sklearn.model_selection import train_test_split

X = df.drop('target', axis=1)
y = df['target']

X_train, X_temp, y_train, y_temp = train_test_split(X, y,
test_size=0.3, random_state=42)
X_val, X_test, y_val, y_test = train_test_split(X_temp, y_temp,
test_size=0.5, random_state=42)
```

Azure ML also supports **cross-validation** and time-series **windowing** for structured experiments.

Logging Data and Metrics

During experimentation, it's crucial to log inputs, metrics, and outputs. Azure ML's SDK allows structured logging to experiment runs.

```
from azureml.core import Run

run = Run.get_context()
run.log("rows", df.shape[0])
run.log_list("feature_names", df.columns.tolist())
```

This ensures traceability and reproducibility in experiments.

Running Experiments

Experiments can be initiated from notebooks, pipelines, or scripts. A basic training run looks like:

```
from azureml.core import ScriptRunConfig
from azureml.core import Experiment
from azureml.core.compute import ComputeTarget

compute = ComputeTarget(workspace=ws, name="cpu-cluster")

src = ScriptRunConfig(source_directory='scripts',
                      script='train.py',
                      compute_target=compute)

exp = Experiment(workspace=ws, name='train-iris')
run = exp.submit(src)
run.wait_for_completion(show_output=True)
```

All outputs (model, logs, metrics) are stored in the experiment run.

Experimenting with Notebooks

Azure ML supports interactive development with hosted Jupyter Notebooks. These notebooks run on compute instances and support:

- Python   3.8+

- Conda   environments

- VS   Code   integration

- Git integration

Common workflows:

- Data exploration
- Feature selection
- Model training
- Metric visualization
- Export to pipelines or deployment artifacts

Notebooks are ideal for iterative exploration before moving to automated pipelines.

Managing Dataset Versions

Dataset versioning helps ensure consistent experimentation over time. When registering a dataset:

```
dataset = dataset.register(workspace=ws, name="churn-data", create_new_version=True)
```

You can refer to a specific version:

```
ds_v2 = Dataset.get_by_name(ws, name="churn-data", version=2)
```

This is critical for reproducibility and debugging.

Tools and Libraries for Experimentation

Tool/Library	Purpose
Pandas	Data manipulation and analysis
Scikit-learn	ML algorithms and preprocessing pipelines
Matplotlib/Seaborn	Data visualization

PyCaret	Low-code AutoML experimentation
Optuna	Hyperparameter optimization
DVC	Dataset and model version control
Great Expectations	Data validation and pipeline testing

Azure ML integrates with many of these tools either directly or via custom environments.

Best Practices

- Use **datasets** and **datastores** for reusable, secure data access.
- Profile your data to uncover hidden issues.
- Automate feature extraction with pipelines or functions.
- Version datasets and transformation scripts.
- Record metrics and logs in every experiment.
- Use **git** to track code changes alongside data and model versions.
- Document assumptions and observations during experiments.

Summary

Data preparation is the cornerstone of effective machine learning. Azure Machine Learning offers a suite of tools and processes to streamline the ingestion, profiling, transformation, and experimentation phases. Whether working interactively in notebooks or automating workflows in pipelines, the platform ensures that your data science practices remain scalable, secure, and repeatable.

As you continue building on your prepared datasets, the next section will dive into training and tuning models using various compute resources, algorithm options, and hyperparameter search strategies—key steps in turning clean data into intelligent predictions.

Training, Tuning, and Deploying Models

Once your data is prepared, the next critical phase in the machine learning lifecycle is model training. This involves choosing an appropriate algorithm, defining training parameters, running experiments, and evaluating the model's performance. In Azure Machine Learning, this process is highly flexible and scalable, supporting everything from local experiments to distributed deep learning at enterprise scale.

This section covers the full process of training and tuning models in Azure ML using both code-first and automated approaches. You'll also learn how to operationalize your best-performing models by deploying them as secure, scalable web services using Azure Container Instances (ACI) or Azure Kubernetes Service (AKS).

Training Models in Azure ML

Azure Machine Learning supports a wide range of training methods:

- **Scripted Training** using Python and the AzureML SDK.

- **Notebook-based Training** using Jupyter Notebooks on compute instances.

- **Low-Code Designer Training** via drag-and-drop interface.

- **Automated ML** for algorithm selection and hyperparameter tuning.

- **Distributed Training** across multiple nodes with GPU acceleration.

Regardless of the approach, every training run is tracked, versioned, and reproducible.

Preparing the Training Script

A typical training script (train.py) contains:

- Argument parsing for hyperparameters

- Data loading logic

- Model training and evaluation

- Model saving

- Logging of metrics

Example:

```python
import argparse
import joblib
from sklearn.ensemble import RandomForestClassifier
from sklearn.metrics import accuracy_score
import pandas as pd

parser = argparse.ArgumentParser()
parser.add_argument('--n_estimators', type=int, default=100)
args = parser.parse_args()

df = pd.read_csv('iris.csv')
X = df.drop('species', axis=1)
y = df['species']

model = RandomForestClassifier(n_estimators=args.n_estimators)
model.fit(X, y)

joblib.dump(model, 'model.joblib')
```

Configuring the Experiment

Using the Azure ML SDK, you can configure the environment and training script execution:

```python
from azureml.core import ScriptRunConfig, Environment
from azureml.core import Experiment

env      =      Environment.from_conda_specification(name='my-env',
file_path='env.yml')

src = ScriptRunConfig(source_directory='scripts',
                      script='train.py',
                      arguments=['--n_estimators', 150],
                      environment=env,
                      compute_target='cpu-cluster')

exp = Experiment(workspace=ws, name='rf-training')
run = exp.submit(src)
run.wait_for_completion(show_output=True)
```

All outputs including logs and model files are stored with the run.

Using the Designer for Visual Training

Azure ML Designer allows you to build a pipeline by:

1. Dragging a dataset module.

2. Selecting a training algorithm (e.g., Decision Forest, Logistic Regression).

3. Adding a **Train Model** module and connecting it to a **Split Data** module.

4. Adding a **Score Model** and **Evaluate Model** module.

You can train and test models without writing code, and results are visualized in charts and tables.

Leveraging Automated Machine Learning (AutoML)

AutoML helps you automatically select the best algorithm, preprocessors, and hyperparameters for your dataset.

Steps:

1. Go to **Automated ML** in Azure ML Studio.

2. Create a new experiment and select a dataset.

3. Choose a target column (e.g., churn).

4. Choose a task type (classification, regression, forecasting).

5. Define compute target and exit conditions (max time, iterations).

6. Launch the experiment.

AutoML outputs:

- A leaderboard of all model runs.

- The best model with metrics (accuracy, precision, etc.).

- Downloadable pipelines for reproducibility.

You can also run AutoML via SDK:

```
from azureml.train.automl import AutoMLConfig
from azureml.core.experiment import Experiment

automl_config = AutoMLConfig(
    task='classification',
    primary_metric='AUC_weighted',
    training_data=dataset,
    label_column_name='target',
    n_cross_validations=5,
    compute_target='cpu-cluster',
    experiment_timeout_minutes=30
)

experiment = Experiment(ws, 'automl-exp')
run = experiment.submit(automl_config, show_output=True)
```

Hyperparameter Tuning with HyperDrive

HyperDrive is Azure ML's hyperparameter tuning framework. It supports:

- Random   sampling

- Grid   search

- Bayesian   optimization

- Early   termination

Define a parameter space:

```
from azureml.train.hyperdrive import RandomParameterSampling, choice,
uniform

param_sampling = RandomParameterSampling({
    'n_estimators': choice(50, 100, 150, 200),
    'max_depth': uniform(3, 10)
})
```

Define the estimator and HyperDrive config:

```
from       azureml.train.hyperdrive      import      HyperDriveConfig,
PrimaryMetricGoal

hd_config = HyperDriveConfig(
    run_config=src,
    hyperparameter_sampling=param_sampling,
    primary_metric_name='accuracy',
    primary_metric_goal=PrimaryMetricGoal.MAXIMIZE,
    max_total_runs=20,
    max_concurrent_runs=4
)

hd_run = exp.submit(hd_config)
hd_run.wait_for_completion(show_output=True)
```

After completion, select the best run:

```
best_run = hd_run.get_best_run_by_primary_metric()
best_model       =       best_run.register_model('best_rf_model',
model_path='outputs/model.joblib')
```

Evaluating Models

Evaluate model performance using:

- Accuracy,   precision,   recall,   F1-score   (classification)

- RMSE,   MAE,   R2   (regression)

- Confusion   matrix,   ROC   curve

Log metrics:

```
run.log("accuracy", accuracy_score(y_true, y_pred))
```

Visualize them in Azure ML Studio under the **Experiments** tab or programmatically:

```
metrics = run.get_metrics()
print(metrics)
```

Registering Models

Model registration enables tracking, versioning, and deployment.

```
from azureml.core.model import Model

model = Model.register(workspace=ws,
                       model_path='outputs/model.joblib',
                       model_name='rf-classifier',
                       description='Random     forest     model     for
classification')
```

You can register models from AutoML or HyperDrive runs using `run.register_model()`.

Creating Inference Config and Environment

Define an environment and scoring script (`score.py`):

```
from azureml.core.environment import Environment
from azureml.core.model import InferenceConfig

env = Environment.from_conda_specification(name="inference-env",
file_path="inference.yml")

inference_config = InferenceConfig(entry_script="score.py",
environment=env)
```

Your `score.py` should define two functions: `init()` and `run(input_data)`.

Deploying the Model

Option 1: Deploy to Azure Container Instance (ACI)

```
from azureml.core.webservice import AciWebservice

deployment_config = AciWebservice.deploy_configuration(cpu_cores=1,
memory_gb=1)

service = Model.deploy(workspace=ws,
                       name="rf-classifier-api",
```

```
                        models=[model],
                        inference_config=inference_config,
                        deployment_config=deployment_config)

service.wait_for_deployment(show_output=True)
print(service.scoring_uri)
```

Option 2: Deploy to Azure Kubernetes Service (AKS)

Use this for production workloads needing high availability and autoscaling.

```
from azureml.core.compute import AksCompute, ComputeTarget

aks_config = AksCompute.provisioning_configuration()
aks_target = ComputeTarget.create(ws, "aks-cluster", aks_config)
aks_target.wait_for_completion(show_output=True)

from azureml.core.webservice import AksWebservice

aks_deployment_config =
AksWebservice.deploy_configuration(cpu_cores=2, memory_gb=4)

service = Model.deploy(workspace=ws,
                        name='rf-api-prod',
                        models=[model],
                        inference_config=inference_config,
                        deployment_config=aks_deployment_config,
                        deployment_target=aks_target)

service.wait_for_deployment(show_output=True)
```

Invoking the Model

Use Python or cURL to send data:

```
import requests, json

uri = service.scoring_uri
headers = {"Content-Type": "application/json"}

data = json.dumps({"data": [[5.1, 3.5, 1.4, 0.2]]})
```

```
response = requests.post(uri, data=data, headers=headers)
print(response.json())
```

You can also enable authentication or deploy behind a VNET for added security.

Monitoring and Logging

Azure ML logs:

- Request   counts

- Latency

- Errors

- Custom   logs

Enable Application Insights for advanced monitoring and alerting.

```
service.update(enable_app_insights=True)
```

Use **Azure Monitor**, **Log Analytics**, or **Prometheus + Grafana** for deeper insights.

Summary

Training, tuning, and deploying machine learning models in Azure ML is a streamlined, powerful process. With support for both low-code and code-first paradigms, built-in hyperparameter tuning, AutoML, and one-click deployment options, Azure enables teams to move from data to production AI quickly and responsibly.

By automating experimentation, tracking metrics, and operationalizing models with secure endpoints, you can ensure that your machine learning workflows are both scalable and reproducible. In the next section, we'll focus on monitoring deployed models, managing versions, and ensuring performance in production environments.

Monitoring and Managing Models in Production

Deploying a machine learning model into production is just the beginning. Real-world environments are dynamic—data distributions shift, user behavior evolves, and system constraints fluctuate. As a result, models need continuous monitoring and maintenance to ensure they remain accurate, responsive, and aligned with business goals. Azure Machine

Learning provides a robust suite of tools and practices for managing the operational lifecycle of models once they are live.

This section covers how to monitor deployed models, detect data drift, manage model versions, handle rollback strategies, implement CI/CD for models (MLOps), and ensure auditability and governance of AI in production.

The Need for Model Monitoring

Why monitor models in production?

- **Data Drift**: Real-world data can differ from training data, degrading model performance.

- **Model Decay**: Over time, static models lose relevance and need retraining.

- **Latency and Availability**: Applications require fast, reliable predictions.

- **Compliance**: Regulatory needs demand traceability and audit logs.

- **User Feedback**: Helps identify blind spots and continuously improve accuracy.

Without active monitoring, even high-performing models can silently fail.

Monitoring Infrastructure in Azure ML

Azure Machine Learning integrates with several services to provide a comprehensive monitoring solution:

- **Application Insights**: Logs request latency, errors, and usage stats.

- **Azure Monitor**: Tracks metrics, performance, and custom logs.

- **Log Analytics**: Centralized query and analysis engine for log data.

- **Data Drift Monitor**: Detects shifts in data distributions.

- **Model Registry**: Tracks versions, lineage, and deployment history.

Enabling Application Insights

When deploying a model, enable telemetry:

```
service.update(enable_app_insights=True)
```

This logs:

- Request count
- Response time
- Success/failure rate
- User-defined logs (e.g., input/output)

View insights:

- In the Azure ML Studio: **Endpoints** > **Monitoring**
- In Azure Portal: **Application Insights** > **Logs**

You can also export logs to a SIEM or monitoring platform like Grafana.

Implementing Custom Logging

You can add custom telemetry inside your scoring script (score.py):

```python
import logging
import json
from azureml.core.model import Model

def init():
    global model
    model_path = Model.get_model_path("my-model")
    logging.info("Model loaded from " + model_path)

def run(data):
    try:
        input_data = json.loads(data)['data']
        result = model.predict(input_data)
        logging.info("Prediction completed.")
        return result.tolist()
```

```
except Exception as e:
    logging.error("Error in prediction: " + str(e))
    return str(e)
```

These logs will be visible in Application Insights and accessible through Kusto queries in Log Analytics.

Data Drift Detection

Azure ML's **Data Drift Monitor** automatically tracks statistical changes in input data over time.

Steps to Configure:

1. Register two datasets:

    ○ **Baseline** (e.g., training data)

    ○ **Target** (e.g., production data over time)

2. In Azure ML Studio:

    ○ Go to **Dataset Monitor**

    ○ Create a new monitor

    ○ Select baseline and target

    ○ Define time window (daily, weekly)

3. Metrics Monitored:

    ○ Feature-wise distribution drift

    ○ KL divergence

    ○ Population stability index (PSI)

    ○ Missing value changes

Alerts can be configured to notify data scientists or trigger automated retraining.

Managing Model Versions

Each model registered in Azure ML is versioned. This allows:

- Easy rollback to a previous version
- Side-by-side comparison of performance
- Controlled promotion from staging to production

Viewing Versions

```
from azureml.core.model import Model

models = Model.list(ws, name='rf-classifier')
for m in models:
    print(m.version, m.id, m.created_time)
```

Promoting a New Model

Update a deployment:

```
service.update(models=[new_model],
inference_config=inference_config)
```

Azure ML supports **blue-green deployments**, enabling canary rollouts for A/B testing.

Auditing and Governance

All actions in Azure ML—training, registration, deployment—are logged for audit purposes.

You can:

- Trace a deployed model back to its source data and code.
- View lineage graphs in the **Model Details** pane.
- Enforce security using **Role-Based Access Control (RBAC)**.

Enable **Azure Policy** to restrict actions (e.g., only deploy models from certified workspaces).

CI/CD and MLOps Integration

CI/CD automates the deployment and monitoring of ML models. Azure ML integrates with:

- **Azure DevOps Pipelines**

- **GitHub Actions**

- **Jenkins and GitLab CI**

A typical ML pipeline includes:

1. **Trigger**: Code/data change
2. **Build**: Lint, test, package code
3. **Train**: Run experiment
4. **Evaluate**: Compare performance with current production model
5. **Register**: Store best model
6. **Deploy**: Update endpoint if better model is found
7. **Monitor**: Track usage and drift

Example GitHub Action:

```
jobs:
  build-train-deploy:
    runs-on: ubuntu-latest
    steps:
      - uses: actions/checkout@v2
      - name: Setup Python
        uses: actions/setup-python@v2
        with:
          python-version: '3.9'
      - name: Install dependencies
        run: pip install -r requirements.txt
      - name: Train and register model
        run: python train_and_register.py
      - name: Deploy to endpoint
        run: python deploy.py
```

Use `azureml-core`, `azureml-mlflow`, or `az ml` CLI for scripting these steps.

Alerting and Recovery

Set up alerts using Azure Monitor:

- Failure rate exceeds threshold

- Latency increases beyond SLA

- Drift score crosses threshold

Send alerts to:

- Email

- Azure Logic App

- Slack/Teams webhook

- ServiceNow ticket

Use **automatic rollback** or **auto-retrain** pipelines in response to alerts.

Shadow Testing and A/B Deployment

To minimize risk during model updates:

- **Shadow Testing**: Send live traffic to a new model but don't expose results to users.

- **A/B Testing**: Split traffic (e.g., 80/20) to evaluate new model performance.

Configure routing via inference endpoints:

```
service.update(traffic={"v1": 80, "v2": 20})
```

Analyze differences in performance using logged metrics and customer feedback.

Scaling and Reliability

Use **Azure Kubernetes Service (AKS)** for production-grade hosting:

- Auto-scaling

- GPU   support

- Private   endpoints

- VNET   integration

Define scaling configuration:

```
from azureml.core.webservice import AksWebservice

deployment_config = AksWebservice.deploy_configuration(
    autoscale_enabled=True,
    autoscale_min_replicas=2,
    autoscale_max_replicas=10,
    cpu_cores=2,
    memory_gb=4
)
```

Monitor performance using Azure Monitor and set SLAs for latency and uptime.

Summary

Monitoring and managing models in production is essential for ensuring sustained business value, reliability, and compliance. Azure Machine Learning provides powerful, integrated tools to track model performance, detect anomalies, manage versions, automate rollouts, and ensure robust governance.

With capabilities like data drift detection, logging via Application Insights, versioned deployments, and CI/CD integration, you can maintain a modern, resilient AI infrastructure that continuously learns and adapts to real-world conditions.

In the next chapter, we'll shift our focus to integrating these intelligent models into web and mobile applications—bridging the gap between model outputs and end-user experiences.

Chapter 5: Integrating AI with Web and Mobile Applications

Using Azure Functions for AI-Driven Workflows

Azure Functions is a serverless compute service that enables developers to run event-driven code without having to manage infrastructure. It is ideally suited for integrating AI services into applications, particularly when building scalable, event-based workflows that consume minimal resources until invoked. Whether calling machine learning models, transforming input/output data, processing images or audio, or coordinating multi-step AI pipelines, Azure Functions offers a lightweight and cost-effective mechanism.

This section explores how to build, deploy, and integrate Azure Functions to invoke AI services such as Azure Machine Learning endpoints, Cognitive Services, or custom models. You will learn how to use triggers, bindings, HTTP endpoints, and environment variables to create robust AI-powered serverless applications.

Why Use Azure Functions for AI Integration?

Serverless architecture offers key advantages for AI-driven apps:

- **Cost efficiency**: You only pay for execution time, not for idle compute.

- **Scalability**: Automatically scales to handle concurrent executions.

- **Low latency**: Ideal for simple and stateless workloads such as real-time inference.

- **Integration-ready**: Easily connects to APIs, storage, queues, and databases.

- **DevOps-friendly**: Supports CI/CD, environment separation, and versioning.

This makes Azure Functions perfect for triggering ML models on-demand (e.g., image analysis after upload, sentiment scoring of a comment, language translation of a post).

Core Concepts

Azure Functions operate based on the following:

- **Triggers**: Define how the function is invoked (e.g., HTTP request, blob creation, queue message).

- **Bindings**: Connect to input/output sources like Azure Storage, Cosmos DB, Event Hubs.

- **Function App**: A container for one or more functions, sharing configuration and environment.

Creating a Basic AI Function

Let's create a function that calls a deployed machine learning model to predict customer churn.

Step 1: Install Tools

Install the Azure Functions Core Tools and create a Python virtual environment:

```
npm install -g azure-functions-core-tools@4 --unsafe-perm true
python -m venv .venv
source .venv/bin/activate
func init ai-functions --python
cd ai-functions
func new --name churnPredictor --template "HTTP trigger" --authlevel
"anonymous"
```

Step 2: Add Model Invocation Code

Edit churnPredictor/__init__.py:

```
import logging
import json
import requests

def main(req):
    try:
        req_body = req.get_json()
        data = req_body['data']

        response = requests.post(
            url="https://<your-service>.azurewebsites.net/score",
            headers={"Content-Type": "application/json"},
            data=json.dumps({"data": data})
        )
```

```
        return {
            'statusCode': 200,
            'body': response.json()
        }

    except Exception as e:
        logging.error(str(e))
        return {
            'statusCode': 500,
            'body': str(e)
        }
```

Step 3: Add Configuration

Store secrets in `local.settings.json`:

```
{
  "IsEncrypted": false,
  "Values": {
    "AzureWebJobsStorage": "UseDevelopmentStorage=true",
    "FUNCTIONS_WORKER_RUNTIME": "python",
    "MODEL_URL": "https://<model-url>.azurewebsites.net/score"
  }
}
```

Access them with `os.environ.get("MODEL_URL")`.

Deploying to Azure

Login to Azure CLI and create a Function App:

```
az login
az functionapp create --resource-group ai-app-rg \
  --consumption-plan-location eastus \
  --runtime python \
  --runtime-version 3.9 \
  --functions-version 4 \
  --name churn-ai-fn \
  --storage-account mystorageaccount
```

Deploy your function:

```
func azure functionapp publish churn-ai-fn
```

Now your function is live and accessible at:

```
https://churn-ai-fn.azurewebsites.net/api/churnPredictor
```

Event-Driven AI with Triggers

Azure Functions can respond to events, making them ideal for workflow automation. Example use cases:

- **Blob Trigger**: Run OCR on a new image in storage.

- **Queue Trigger**: Translate and store text messages from users.

- **Timer Trigger**: Periodically score new data and flag anomalies.

Example: OCR on Blob Upload

Create a Blob Triggered Function:

```
func new --name processImage --template "Blob trigger"
```

Edit processImage/__init__.py:

```python
import azure.functions as func
import requests

def main(myblob: func.InputStream):
    image_bytes = myblob.read()
    headers = {
        'Ocp-Apim-Subscription-Key': '<vision-key>',
        'Content-Type': 'application/octet-stream'
    }

    response = requests.post(

url="https://<region>.api.cognitive.microsoft.com/vision/v3.2/read/analyze",
```

```
        headers=headers,
        data=image_bytes
    )

    print("OCR initiated:", response.status_code)
```

Using Functions with Pipelines

Azure Functions are lightweight and modular, making them ideal for **chaining workflows**:

- Upload → Trigger preprocessing

- Preprocess → Trigger inference

- Inference → Trigger post-processing

- Post-process → Save and log result

You can chain these via Azure Queues or Event Grid.

Logging and Monitoring

Azure Functions integrates with Application Insights:

```
az monitor diagnostic-settings create \
  --resource churn-ai-fn \
  --workspace <log-analytics-id> \
  --logs '[{"category":"FunctionAppLogs","enabled":true}]'
```

You can:

- Log execution durations

- View exceptions

- Trace HTTP responses

- Create alerts on failure rates or error counts

Use Kusto queries to analyze logs:

```
requests
| where cloud_RoleName == "churn-ai-fn"
| summarize avg(duration) by bin(timestamp, 1h)
```

Scaling Considerations

Functions scale based on trigger type:

- **HTTP**: Instantly scales with incoming requests.
- **Blob/Queue**: Scales with item count.
- **Timer**: Executes on schedule.

For production:

- Enable **Always On** for premium plans.
- Use **Dedicated Plans** for high throughput.
- Optimize **cold start** by minimizing dependencies.

Secure AI Integration

Use the following for secure deployments:

- **Managed Identity**: Allow functions to securely call other Azure resources.
- **Key Vault**: Store and retrieve secrets.
- **RBAC**: Limit access to inference endpoints and storage accounts.
- **CORS**: Restrict HTTP calls to approved domains.

Add Key Vault reference:

```
from azure.identity import DefaultAzureCredential
from azure.keyvault.secrets import SecretClient
```

```
credential = DefaultAzureCredential()
client = SecretClient(vault_url="https://<vault>.vault.azure.net/",
credential=credential)
api_key = client.get_secret("model-api-key").value
```

Real-World Use Cases

Use Case	Trigger	Description
Image tagging on upload	Blob Trigger	Detect objects and tag new photos
Chatbot message translation	Queue Trigger	Translate user input before reply
Fraud alert scoring	HTTP/Timer Trigger	Run ML scoring model on new transactions
Document OCR and storage	Blob Trigger	Extract and save text from PDFs
Customer review sentiment analysis	HTTP Trigger	Score sentiment in real-time from API

Best Practices

- Keep functions **stateless** and **idempotent**.
- Use **managed identities** for secure, passwordless access.
- Set **timeouts** **and** **retries** for long-running calls.
- Handle **errors** **and** **exceptions** gracefully with logging and alerting.
- Use **queues** to decouple logic and smooth load.

Summary

Azure Functions provide a highly effective way to embed AI capabilities into applications with minimal code and infrastructure. Whether you're invoking pre-trained Cognitive Services, calling custom machine learning models, or building multi-stage AI pipelines, Functions offer a serverless backbone that's scalable, event-driven, and cost-efficient.

In the next section, we'll explore how to embed these AI-powered services directly into web applications using JavaScript and .NET—bringing intelligence closer to the end user in real time.

Embedding AI in Web Applications with JavaScript and .NET

Web applications serve as the primary interface for most AI-powered solutions. Whether it's delivering intelligent recommendations, enabling natural language interactions, or analyzing uploaded images, integrating AI into web applications allows users to experience the power of machine learning and cognitive services in real time. Azure provides a flexible and scalable foundation for embedding these intelligent features through REST APIs, SDKs, and serverless backends that can be consumed from both JavaScript and .NET applications.

This section explores techniques for integrating Azure AI capabilities—such as Cognitive Services, Azure Machine Learning endpoints, and AI search—into web applications built with modern JavaScript frameworks (React, Vue, Angular) and ASP.NET Core. We'll cover frontend and backend communication, authentication, real-time updates, performance optimization, and deployment best practices.

Use Cases for AI in Web Apps

Use Case	AI Capability Used
Image classification and tagging	Computer Vision API, Custom Vision
Sentiment analysis of user comments	Text Analytics API
Product search and recommendations	Azure Cognitive Search with AI enrichment
Language translation of messages	Azure Translator
Face verification during login	Face API
Predictive form completion	Custom ML models deployed via Azure ML

Architecture Overview

To integrate AI into a web app, a typical architecture involves:

- **Frontend (React/Angular/HTML)**: Collects user input, displays results.

- **Backend (Node.js/.NET)**: Acts as a proxy between frontend and Azure AI services.

- **Azure AI Services**: Provides prediction, analysis, or data enrichment.

- **Azure Functions or Web API**: Handles logic, API calls, and authentication.

- **Azure App Service or Static Web Apps**: Hosts the frontend securely.

Calling Azure AI Services from JavaScript

Azure Cognitive Services are exposed as RESTful APIs. You can call them directly from the frontend using `fetch`, Axios, or similar tools.

Example: Sentiment Analysis with JavaScript

```
async function analyzeSentiment(text) {
  const endpoint =
"https://<region>.api.cognitive.microsoft.com/text/analytics/v3.1/se
ntiment";
  const apiKey = "<your-api-key>";

  const response = await fetch(endpoint, {
    method: "POST",
    headers: {
      "Ocp-Apim-Subscription-Key": apiKey,
      "Content-Type": "application/json"
    },
    body: JSON.stringify({
      documents: [
        { id: "1", language: "en", text: text }
      ]
    })
  });

  const result = await response.json();
  return result.documents[0].sentiment;
}
```

Render results in React:

```
const [sentiment, setSentiment] = useState(null);

const handleSubmit = async () => {
  const userInput = document.getElementById("text").value;
  const result = await analyzeSentiment(userInput);
  setSentiment(result);
};
```

Securing API Keys

Never expose your keys in frontend code for production environments.

Best practices:

- Use a backend (Azure Function, Express, .NET Web API) to proxy requests.

- Store keys in environment variables or Azure Key Vault.

- Use Azure AD for secure token-based access to resources.

Invoking Azure ML Models from Web Frontends

If you've deployed a model to Azure ML, you can call its scoring endpoint from your web backend.

Frontend: Send data to your API

```
fetch('/api/predict', {
  method: 'POST',
  headers: { 'Content-Type': 'application/json' },
  body: JSON.stringify({ data: [userInput] })
})
  .then(res => res.json())
  .then(result => display(result));
```

Backend: Call the Azure ML endpoint (.NET)

```
[ApiController]
[Route("api/[controller]")]
public class PredictController : ControllerBase
{
```

```
    [HttpPost]
    public async Task<IActionResult> Post([FromBody] PredictionInput
input)
    {
        var client = new HttpClient();
        client.DefaultRequestHeaders.Add("Authorization",    "Bearer
YOUR_API_KEY");

        var payload = new
        {
            data = input.Data
        };

        var                 content                 =                 new
StringContent(JsonConvert.SerializeObject(payload),    Encoding.UTF8,
"application/json");
        var    response    =    await    client.PostAsync("https://<ml-
endpoint>/score", content);

        var result = await response.Content.ReadAsStringAsync();
        return Ok(result);
    }
}
```

Using Azure SDKs in .NET

Azure offers comprehensive SDKs for .NET. Example: Text Analytics

```
var    client    =    new    TextAnalyticsClient(new    Uri(endpoint),    new
AzureKeyCredential(apiKey));
var response = await client.AnalyzeSentimentAsync("I love using this
app!");
Console.WriteLine($"Sentiment: {response.Value.Sentiment}");
```

Integrate this into an ASP.NET Core controller and expose via API to frontend.

Real-Time AI with SignalR and WebSockets

For dynamic interfaces like chatbots, dashboards, or live updates, use **SignalR** to stream AI results.

Use Case: Real-time OCR with SignalR

1. User uploads image.

2. Frontend sends to backend via SignalR.

3. Backend processes with Computer Vision OCR.

4. Streams back recognized text to client.

Performance and UX Considerations

To ensure a responsive user experience:

- **Debounce inputs** for NLP/translation tasks.

- **Show loading indicators** while awaiting AI responses.

- **Batch API calls** where possible.

- **Use async/await** or promises to avoid UI blocking.

- **Paginate or filter results** when working with AI search.

Deployment Options

For JavaScript Frontends:

- Use **Azure Static Web Apps** with GitHub Actions CI/CD.

- Host in **Azure App Service** for SSR frameworks (e.g., Next.js).

- Secure endpoints with **Azure Front Door**, **API Management**, or **Azure AD B2C**.

For .NET Apps:

- Deploy backend via **Azure App Service** or **AKS**.

- Use **Application** **Insights** for telemetry.

- Manage environments with **App** **Configuration** or **Key** **Vault**.

Real-World Implementation Patterns

Pattern	Description	Example
Serverless AI Proxy	Frontend sends request to Azure Function which then calls AI service	Sentiment API via Function App
Hybrid App	Frontend in React, backend in ASP.NET Core, both deployed on App Service	ML prediction with secured backend
Embedded Intelligence	Use JavaScript SDKs to analyze content locally before sending	Content moderation in chat app
Real-Time Streaming	Use SignalR or WebSocket to push updates from AI backend	Live transcription dashboard

Best Practices

- Abstract AI calls into reusable services.

- Use structured models for API inputs/outputs.

- Secure your APIs—never expose secret keys.

- Version your AI endpoints for backward compatibility.

- Monitor AI usage and response quality over time.

- Test with varied, real-world inputs to improve UX.

Summary

Integrating AI into web applications using JavaScript and .NET unlocks smarter, more responsive user experiences. With Azure's RESTful APIs and SDKs, you can quickly add capabilities like translation, image recognition, sentiment analysis, and custom ML inference to your applications—while maintaining scalability, security, and maintainability.

Whether building a simple sentiment detector or a full-fledged intelligent assistant, Azure's ecosystem enables you to deliver these features seamlessly to end users. In the next section, we'll explore how to extend this power to mobile platforms using Xamarin and Flutter for native-like, cross-platform AI experiences.

Creating AI-Powered Mobile Apps with Xamarin and Flutter

The rise of mobile computing has transformed how users interact with intelligent systems. As mobile applications become the primary interface for users around the world, integrating artificial intelligence (AI) into mobile apps enables rich, personalized, and intuitive experiences. Whether through voice-enabled assistants, real-time image recognition, language translation, or predictive analytics, AI has become a cornerstone of modern mobile development.

Azure provides robust services and SDKs that integrate seamlessly with cross-platform frameworks like **Xamarin** and **Flutter**, enabling developers to build AI-powered mobile apps without managing complex machine learning infrastructure. This section explores how to incorporate Azure Cognitive Services, Azure Machine Learning, and other AI capabilities into mobile apps built with Xamarin (C#) and Flutter (Dart), covering architecture, authentication, performance, offline handling, and deployment.

Why Use Xamarin and Flutter?

Xamarin and **Flutter** are popular frameworks for building cross-platform mobile apps with native performance:

Framework	Language	Highlights
Xamarin	C#/.NET	Mature .NET ecosystem, native bindings, MVVM
Flutter	Dart	Fast UI development, widget-based, high performance

Both platforms can invoke REST APIs, integrate with native libraries, and utilize Azure SDKs or HTTP clients to communicate with AI services.

AI Features for Mobile Apps

Feature	Azure Service
Real-time speech-to-text	Azure Speech
Face detection in camera feed	Computer Vision, Face API
Document OCR from photos	Azure Read API
Sentiment analysis of input	Text Analytics
Language translation	Azure Translator
Predictive text suggestions	Azure Machine Learning
Voice commands and responses	Speech + Language + TTS APIs

Architecture Overview

A typical AI-powered mobile app includes:

- **Frontend (Xamarin/Flutter)**: UI, sensor integration (camera, mic), API calls.
- **Backend**: Optional Azure Functions or Web APIs to proxy or preprocess requests.
- **AI Services**: Azure-hosted cognitive or ML models.
- **Storage**: Azure Blob, Cosmos DB, SQLite (offline caching).
- **Authentication**: Azure AD B2C or MSAL for secure access.

You can choose direct API invocation or route traffic through a secured serverless backend.

Calling Azure AI Services from Xamarin

In Xamarin, you can use `HttpClient` to call REST APIs or the Azure SDKs for selected services.

Example: Analyzing Image Tags with Computer Vision

```
using System.Net.Http;
```

```
using System.Text;
using Newtonsoft.Json;

public async Task<string> AnalyzeImageAsync(string imageUrl)
{
    var client = new HttpClient();
    client.DefaultRequestHeaders.Add("Ocp-Apim-Subscription-Key",
"<your-key>");

    var requestBody = JsonConvert.SerializeObject(new { url = imageUrl
});
    var content = new StringContent(requestBody, Encoding.UTF8,
"application/json");

    var response = await
client.PostAsync("https://<region>.api.cognitive.microsoft.com/visio
n/v3.2/analyze?visualFeatures=Tags", content);
    return await response.Content.ReadAsStringAsync();
}
```

Bind the result to your UI using MVVM.

Calling Azure AI Services from Flutter

In Flutter, use http or dio packages to send requests to Azure endpoints.

Example: Translate Text with Azure Translator

```
import 'package:http/http.dart' as http;
import 'dart:convert';

Future<String> translateText(String input) async {
  final response = await http.post(

Uri.parse('https://api.cognitive.microsofttranslator.com/translate?a
pi-version=3.0&to=fr'),
    headers: {
      'Ocp-Apim-Subscription-Key': '<your-key>',
      'Content-Type': 'application/json',
      'X-ClientTraceId': '<uuid>'
    },
```

```
  body: json.encode([{ 'Text': input }]),
);

final data = json.decode(response.body);
return data[0]['translations'][0]['text'];
}
```

Update the UI using FutureBuilder or reactive state management (e.g., Bloc, Riverpod).

Using Azure Machine Learning in Mobile Apps

For custom models deployed in Azure ML, expose a REST endpoint:

- Input: JSON   with   feature   values

- Output: Prediction   results

Flutter/Xamarin Calling ML Model

```
final response = await http.post(
  Uri.parse('https://<ml-endpoint>.azurewebsites.net/score'),
  headers: {
    'Content-Type': 'application/json',
    'Authorization': 'Bearer <your-key>'
  },
  body: jsonEncode({'data': [[input1, input2, input3]]})
);
```

Results can be used to drive recommendations, personalization, or predictions.

Offline Capabilities and Edge Scenarios

Mobile environments often experience intermittent connectivity. To maintain usability:

- Cache predictions and results using **SQLite** or **Hive** (Flutter) / **SQLite.NET** (Xamarin).

- Store   recent   images   and   queue   for   later   upload.

- Use **on-device inference** via models exported to **ONNX**, **TensorFlow Lite**, or **Core ML**.

You can deploy selected models as **Azure Percept** or **IoT Edge** modules for offline environments.

Authentication with Azure AD B2C

To securely access Azure AI services:

1. Register your mobile app in Azure AD B2C.

2. Integrate the **MSAL** (Microsoft Authentication Library).

Xamarin Authentication

```
var pca = PublicClientApplicationBuilder.Create(clientId)
    .WithB2CAuthority(authority)
    .WithRedirectUri("msal<your-client-id>://auth")
    .Build();

var result = await
pca.AcquireTokenInteractive(scopes).ExecuteAsync();
```

Flutter Authentication

Use `msal_flutter` or `flutter_appauth`:

```
final AuthorizationTokenResponse? result = await
appAuth.authorizeAndExchangeCode(
  AuthorizationTokenRequest(
    clientId,
    redirectUrl,
    discoveryUrl: discoveryUrl,
    scopes: ['openid', 'profile', 'offline_access']
  )
);
```

Use the token to call secure endpoints.

Performance Optimization

To ensure responsive UX:

- **Use background isolates** or threads to process heavy computations.

- **Compress images** before uploading.

- **Throttle requests** using debounce or rate limits.

- **Use caching** for repeated queries or content (images, tags).

- **Optimize builds** (AOT for Flutter, Release mode for Xamarin).

Deployment and DevOps

Use the following tools for CI/CD:

- **Xamarin**: Azure DevOps Pipelines + App Center.

- **Flutter**: GitHub Actions + Firebase App Distribution or App Store Connect.

Monitor app usage and errors via:

- **App Center**

- **Firebase Analytics**

- **Azure Monitor + Application Insights**

Log AI interactions for continual improvement and debugging.

Real-World Scenarios

App Type	AI Use Case
Language Learning	Speech-to-text, translation, TTS
Retail Loyalty App	Personalized offers via ML predictions
Accessibility Tools	OCR + Text-to-Speech for visual assistance
Fitness/Health App	Pose detection or audio coaching using AI

| Field Service App | Equipment scanning and tagging with Custom Vision |
| Chat and Messaging | Sentiment and language detection with real-time response |

Best Practices

- **Isolate AI logic** into services or providers for maintainability.
- Always **handle errors gracefully** and provide user feedback.
- Use **secure, token-based communication**—never embed secrets.
- Keep models **versioned** and use feature flags for experimental features.
- Monitor **user feedback** and logs to refine AI performance.
- Always test with **diverse datasets** to reduce bias and ensure fairness.

Summary

Xamarin and Flutter, when combined with Azure AI services, empower developers to deliver intelligent, responsive, and personalized mobile experiences. Whether you need real-time translation, facial recognition, predictive recommendations, or voice assistance, Azure provides a scalable and secure backend while Xamarin and Flutter offer rich cross-platform development tools.

By adopting clean architectures, secure communication, offline handling, and continuous delivery, you can bring AI from the cloud to your users' pockets—enabling smarter apps that evolve with every interaction.

Next, we'll focus on ensuring these AI features remain scalable and performant under real-world production conditions—crucial for maintaining seamless user experiences at scale.

Ensuring Scalability and Performance

As AI-powered applications evolve and attract more users, ensuring they scale effectively and maintain optimal performance becomes essential. Scalability is the ability of a system to handle increasing workloads without compromising responsiveness, while performance refers to the speed and efficiency of serving AI tasks such as inference, training, or data retrieval. Azure provides a comprehensive set of tools, architectural strategies, and services to help developers build AI applications that are fast, resilient, and prepared for production workloads.

This section explores the principles and practical approaches to designing and managing scalable, high-performance AI systems—especially those that are accessed by web and mobile frontends. You'll learn how to leverage serverless computing, caching, load balancing, autoscaling, and edge deployments, as well as best practices for optimizing inference latency, throughput, and cost efficiency.

Scalability in AI Application Architecture

A scalable architecture for AI-powered applications typically consists of:

- **Frontend**: JavaScript, Flutter, or Xamarin app.

- **API Gateway**: Azure API Management or Azure Front Door.

- **Backend**: Azure Functions, App Services, or AKS.

- **AI Services**: Azure Cognitive Services or Azure Machine Learning endpoints.

- **Data Storage**: Cosmos DB, Azure Blob, SQL Database.

- **Monitoring**: Application Insights and Azure Monitor.

Each component should be independently scalable, stateless (where possible), and resilient to spikes in traffic.

Key Factors That Impact Scalability

Factor	Impact	Optimization Strategy
Model complexity	Increases inference latency	Use lighter models, quantize, use ONNX
Request volume	Overloads API/backend	Load balance, autoscale, cache responses
Data size	Slows down I/O operations	Batch requests, index search content
Cold starts (serverless)	Causes latency spikes	Use premium tiers, reduce dependency footprint

| Authentication overhead | Adds time to each request | Cache tokens, minimize round trips |

Optimizing Model Inference Performance

Reduce Payload Size

- Compress input images before sending to Vision APIs.

- Send only necessary features in JSON payloads.

- Avoid verbose metadata in API responses.

Use ONNX Runtime

ONNX (Open Neural Network Exchange) allows you to export and optimize models for fast inference across platforms.

```
import onnxruntime as ort

session = ort.InferenceSession("model.onnx")
results = session.run(None, {"input": input_array})
```

ONNX Runtime supports CPU, GPU, and even edge accelerators, delivering 2x–5x speedup in many cases.

Model Quantization

Convert floating-point models to lower precision (e.g., INT8) to reduce memory and compute requirements.

Benefits:

- Smaller model size

- Faster inference

- Lower power usage (great for mobile and IoT)

Autoscaling with Azure Services

Azure Functions

- **Consumption Plan**: Scales automatically based on request load.

- **Premium Plan**: Eliminates cold start, supports VNET integration.

```
az functionapp plan update --name myplan --resource-group mygroup --max-burst 20
```

Azure Kubernetes Service (AKS)

Use Horizontal Pod Autoscaler (HPA) for model deployments:

```
apiVersion: autoscaling/v2
kind: HorizontalPodAutoscaler
spec:
  scaleTargetRef:
    apiVersion: apps/v1
    kind: Deployment
    name: model-api
  minReplicas: 2
  maxReplicas: 10
  metrics:
  - type: Resource
    resource:
      name: cpu
      target:
        type: Utilization
        averageUtilization: 60
```

AKS also supports GPU nodes for large model deployments.

Azure App Service

Scale automatically based on:

- CPU   usage

- Memory   usage

- HTTP   queue   length

- Scheduled rules (e.g., scale up during business hours)

Load Balancing and Caching

Load Balancing

Use **Azure Front Door** or **Application Gateway**:

- Geo-distribution

- SSL   offloading

- Request   routing   by   path,   region,   or   latency

This ensures high availability and low latency for global users.

Caching Results

Use **Azure Cache for Redis**:

- Cache   frequent   AI   results   (e.g.,   same   image   tags).

- Store   user   sessions   or   tokenized   data.

Example (Python):

```python
import redis
r = redis.Redis(host='redis-server', port=6379)
cached_result = r.get(image_hash)

if not cached_result:
    result = call_vision_api(image_url)
    r.set(image_hash, json.dumps(result))
else:
    result = json.loads(cached_result)
```

Caching dramatically reduces duplicate calls to Cognitive Services or ML endpoints.

Parallel and Batch Inference

Batch Processing

Send multiple records at once to reduce overhead:

```
{
  "data": [
    ["input1", "input2", "input3"],
    ["inputA", "inputB", "inputC"]
  ]
}
```

Batching is particularly effective when calling custom models hosted in Azure ML or AKS.

Parallel Execution

Use asyncio (Python) or background threads (C#, Dart) to process multiple requests simultaneously:

```
import asyncio

async def score(input):
    return await call_model(input)

results = await asyncio.gather(*[score(i) for i in inputs])
```

Monitoring and Alerting for Performance

Application Insights

Track:

- Response   time

- Success   rate

- Exception   traces

- Custom   metrics   (e.g.,   confidence   scores,   processing   time)

Create alerts when:

- Latency   exceeds   threshold

- Failure   rate   spikes

- Request   volume   drops   unexpectedly

Azure Monitor

Use for system-level metrics:

- CPU/GPU   utilization

- Network   I/O

- Memory   pressure

- Disk   queue   length

Dashboards help visualize trends and make informed scaling decisions.

Edge Computing for Low Latency

Deploy models close to users using:

- **Azure**   **IoT**   **Edge**

- **Azure**   **Stack**   **Edge**

- **ONNX**   **Runtime**   **Mobile**

- **TFLite**   **on**   **Android/iOS**

Benefits:

- Ultra-low   latency   (<10   ms)

- Offline   processing

- Reduced   bandwidth   and   cloud   costs

Use cases:

- Retail   kiosks

- Smart   cameras

- Industrial   IoT

- AR/VR   experiences

Security and Isolation for Scaling

- **Use Azure Private Link** to restrict AI endpoints to internal networks.
- **API Management** to throttle and secure public access.
- **Rate limiting** for external clients using API keys or OAuth scopes.
- **Isolate workloads** with containerized models and separate namespaces.

Cost Optimization Strategies

Area	Strategy
API usage	Cache frequent calls, batch inputs
Model hosting	Use serverless for low-frequency endpoints
Compute resources	Use spot VMs or auto-scaling for training
Model complexity	Use distilled or quantized models
Storage costs	Clean up unused logs, versioned models

Monitor usage and set budget alerts using **Azure Cost Management**.

Summary

Scalability and performance are critical for delivering seamless AI experiences, especially when deployed at scale across devices and regions. With Azure's rich set of tools—from autoscaling infrastructure to intelligent caching and monitoring—you can ensure your AI-powered applications remain fast, resilient, and cost-effective.

By designing with scalability in mind and continuously monitoring real-world performance, developers can confidently serve growing user bases without compromising on speed or quality. In the next chapter, we'll turn our attention to data strategy and AI pipelines—ensuring your models are continuously fueled by high-quality, well-governed data.

Chapter 6: Data Strategy and AI Pipelines in Azure

Data Lakes and Azure Data Factory

In any AI application, data is the lifeblood. From training and testing machine learning models to feeding real-time analytics and inference systems, managing data at scale is a complex but essential endeavor. Azure offers a powerful combination of tools to meet this challenge— **Azure Data Lake Storage** for scalable, secure, and hierarchical data storage, and **Azure Data Factory** for orchestration of data movement and transformation pipelines. Together, these tools form the backbone of an effective AI data strategy.

This section covers how to architect and implement data lakes and pipelines in Azure specifically for AI workloads. We'll walk through data lake design patterns, ingestion techniques, transformation pipelines, integration with AI services, and best practices for governance, cost optimization, and scalability.

What Is a Data Lake?

A data lake is a centralized repository that allows you to store all your structured and unstructured data at any scale. Unlike traditional data warehouses, data lakes accept raw data in its native format and allow schema to be applied only when the data is read (schema-on-read).

Azure provides a modern implementation of this with **Azure Data Lake Storage Gen2 (ADLS Gen2)**, built on top of Blob Storage and enhanced with big data capabilities.

Key features:

- Hierarchical namespace for file and directory structures
- Massive scalability and high throughput
- Integration with analytics tools (Spark, Synapse, Databricks)
- Fine-grained security and access control via Azure RBAC and ACLs
- Native support for Hadoop-compatible tools

Designing a Data Lake for AI Workloads

A well-organized data lake typically follows a **multi-zone architecture**:

Zone	Purpose
Raw	Stores ingested data in native formats
Staged	Holds data undergoing cleansing or format conversion
Curated	Final, cleaned, enriched datasets for consumption
Reference	External or static reference datasets (lookups)
Sandbox	Experimental or exploratory data for prototyping

Folder path example:

```
/data-lake/
  └── raw/
      └── sensor/2025/04/24/
  └── staged/
      └── sensor-cleaned/
  └── curated/
      └── machine-learning/train/
  └── reference/
      └── iso-country-codes.csv
```

Use metadata tagging and naming conventions to enhance discoverability and automation.

Provisioning Azure Data Lake Storage

Create an ADLS Gen2 account:

```
az storage account create \
  --name mydatalake \
  --resource-group ai-rg \
  --location eastus \
  --sku Standard_LRS \
```

```
--kind StorageV2 \
--hierarchical-namespace true
```

Assign roles for access:

```
az role assignment create \
  --assignee <user-or-app-id> \
  --role "Storage Blob Data Contributor" \
  --scope                 "/subscriptions/<sub-id>/resourceGroups/ai-
rg/providers/Microsoft.Storage/storageAccounts/mydatalake"
```

Mount the lake to Spark or Databricks:

```
spark.conf.set("fs.azure.account.key.mydatalake.dfs.core.windows.net
", "<access-key>")
df                                                                  =
spark.read.text("abfss://raw@mydatalake.dfs.core.windows.net/sensor/
2025/04/24/")
```

Introducing Azure Data Factory

Azure Data Factory (ADF) is a serverless, cloud-based ETL (Extract, Transform, Load) service that lets you move and transform data from diverse sources to destinations, including data lakes, warehouses, and APIs.

ADF supports:

- 100+ data connectors
- Data flow transformations (no-code and code-first)
- Scheduling and triggers
- Custom pipelines with branching and parameters
- Integration with GitHub and Azure DevOps
- Data lineage and monitoring dashboards

ADF is ideal for orchestrating data pipelines that prepare data for AI training and inference processes.

Creating a Data Ingestion Pipeline with ADF

Suppose you want to ingest IoT sensor data from a SQL database into your data lake for AI analysis.

Step 1: Create Linked Services

- **SQL**   **Database:**   Source

- **Azure**   **Data**   **Lake**   **Gen2:**   Sink

Step 2: Define Datasets

- Source: Table   or   query   from   SQL

- Sink: Folder   path   in   raw   zone   (`/raw/sensor/`)

Step 3: Build a Pipeline

Use the visual interface or ARM templates to create a pipeline that:

1. Connects   to   SQL
2. Copies   data   to   ADLS
3. Appends   timestamped   folder   path
4. Logs   success/failure   status

Example JSON snippet:

```json
"activities": [
  {
    "name": "CopySensorData",
    "type": "Copy",
    "inputs": [ { "referenceName": "SQLDataset" } ],
    "outputs": [ { "referenceName": "ADLSDataset" } ],
    "typeProperties": {
      "source": { "type": "SqlSource" },
      "sink": { "type": "DelimitedTextSink" }
    }
  }
}
```

```
]
```

You can also use parameterized folder paths like:

```
/raw/sensor/@{formatDateTime(utcNow(), 'yyyy/MM/dd')}/
```

Transforming Data with ADF Data Flows

ADF supports **mapping data flows**, which are no-code visual transformations similar to SSIS or Power BI Power Query.

Common transformations:

- Filter

- Conditional   split

- Join

- Derived   column

- Aggregate

- Surrogate   key

For more complex logic, use **Azure Databricks notebooks**, **Spark scripts**, or **Azure Synapse pipelines**.

Integrating AI into Data Pipelines

You can enrich data using AI services during ETL/ELT:

- **Text Analytics**: Detect sentiment or key phrases from feedback data.

- **Computer Vision**: Extract tags and descriptions from images.

- **Custom Models**: Call an Azure ML endpoint from a pipeline activity.

ADF supports **Web Activity** and **Azure ML Activity** to trigger model scoring jobs.

```
{
  "name": "ScoreImage",
```

```
  "type": "WebActivity",
  "typeProperties": {
    "method": "POST",
    "url": "https://<ml-endpoint>/score",
    "headers": {
      "Content-Type": "application/json"
    },
    "body": "{ 'image_url': '@pipeline().parameters.imageUrl' }"
  }
}
```

Scheduling and Triggering Pipelines

You can execute pipelines via:

- **Manual** **trigger**

- **Scheduled** **trigger** (e.g., daily at midnight)

- **Event-based** **trigger** (e.g., blob creation)

- **API** **call** (from app or Azure Logic App)

Example: Trigger a pipeline on new file upload

```
az datafactory trigger create \
  --factory-name my-adf \
  --resource-group ai-rg \
  --name BlobTrigger \
  --type BlobEventsTrigger \
  --blob-path-begins-with "raw/images/"
```

Monitoring and Alerting

Monitor pipeline runs in ADF:

- Visual UI: Success/failure, duration, data size

- Logs: Output per activity

- Integration with **Azure Monitor**, **Log Analytics**, and **Alerts**

Set alerts for:

- Failed pipeline runs
- SLA violations
- Missing or delayed data

Best Practices for Data Lakes and Pipelines

Practice	Recommendation
Folder structure	Use YYYY/MM/DD format and zone-based hierarchy
Access control	Use Azure RBAC + POSIX-style ACLs
Metadata management	Tag datasets with schema, owner, sensitivity
Versioning	Store immutable raw data, apply versioning to curated datasets
File format	Use Parquet or Delta Lake for analytics; avoid CSV for large-scale workloads
Automation	Parameterize pipelines and deploy via DevOps
Cost management	Compress files, optimize frequency of movement

Summary

A solid data lake and pipeline strategy is the foundation of any scalable AI system. Azure Data Lake Storage and Azure Data Factory enable developers to ingest, clean, transform, and enrich data at scale—while ensuring governance, performance, and flexibility. With the right zoning structure, security configuration, and integration with AI services, your data lake becomes a powerhouse for training robust models and serving intelligent applications.

In the next section, we'll examine how to streamline ETL processes specifically for AI use cases—ensuring that the right data is available at the right time, in the right format, to power insights and predictions.

Streamlining ETL for AI Applications

Extract, Transform, Load (ETL) processes are central to AI development. ETL pipelines ensure that data from disparate sources is consolidated, cleaned, transformed, and delivered into a state that machine learning models can consume. Unlike traditional business intelligence applications where ETL feeds static dashboards or reports, AI systems often require continuous, dynamic, and high-quality data to fuel training and inference workflows.

Azure provides powerful tools to design and streamline ETL pipelines tailored to AI needs. These include Azure Data Factory (ADF), Azure Synapse, Azure Databricks, and integration with Azure Machine Learning. In this section, we will explore the strategies, technologies, and practices needed to build fast, scalable, and intelligent ETL pipelines that ensure AI applications remain accurate, efficient, and production-ready.

Unique ETL Requirements for AI

Compared to typical analytics ETL, AI-focused ETL processes need to:

- **Preserve raw data** for retraining and auditability.

- **Support both batch and streaming ingestion**.

- **Handle high-velocity data** from IoT devices, APIs, and logs.

- **Apply feature engineering and transformation during preprocessing**.

- **Enable schema evolution** as new features are introduced.

- **Log and version data** used in model training.

The goal of AI ETL is not just to deliver clean tables—it is to generate **high-quality feature sets** that improve model performance while remaining traceable and reproducible.

Overview of Tools and Services

Tool	Purpose
Azure Data Factory	Orchestrate data flows and pipelines

Azure Databricks	Perform distributed data processing, feature engineering with Spark
Azure Synapse	Query data lakes and warehouses with serverless SQL
Azure Stream Analytics	Real-time transformation of streaming data
Azure ML Pipelines	Integrate data prep directly into ML workflows

Most solutions use a combination of batch and real-time processing, depending on the use case.

Extract: Ingesting Diverse Data Sources

AI systems may consume data from:

- Relational databases (SQL Server, PostgreSQL, MySQL)

- Data lakes (ADLS Gen2, Blob Storage)

- SaaS APIs (Salesforce, Dynamics 365, social media)

- IoT devices (Event Hubs, IoT Hub)

- Web logs, clickstream data, telemetry

Using Azure Data Factory

ADF provides over 100 pre-built connectors for sources and destinations.

Example: Ingest CSV files from an SFTP server to Azure Data Lake

```
{
  "type": "Copy",
  "source": { "type": "DelimitedTextSource" },
  "sink": { "type": "AzureBlobSink" },
  "translator": {
    "type": "TabularTranslator",
    "columnMappings": "id:id,name:name,date:date"
  }
}
```

You can automate extraction with scheduled triggers or event-based triggers (e.g., blob upload).

Transform: Preparing Data for AI Consumption

Transformation in AI is more than cleansing—it involves **engineering features**, handling missing values, encoding variables, and standardizing input formats.

Feature Engineering with Azure Data Flow

Common transformations include:

- **One-hot** **encoding** for categorical variables

- **Bucketing** continuous values

- **Combining** **features** (e.g., age * income)

- **Text** **preprocessing** (tokenization, lowercasing)

- **Image** **transformation** (resizing, normalization)

- **Time-based** **extraction** (hour of day, day of week)

These can be implemented in Azure Data Factory's Mapping Data Flows or in Databricks notebooks using Spark.

Example: Deriving features in PySpark

```
from pyspark.sql.functions import col, when

df = df.withColumn("is_high_income", when(col("income") > 100000, 1).otherwise(0))
df = df.withColumn("log_age", col("age") + 1).withColumn("log_age", log("log_age"))
```

These features can be saved to Parquet files or a Delta Lake table for reuse.

Load: Delivering AI-Ready Datasets

Once transformed, data should be loaded into a format suitable for:

- Training ML models (tabular, vectorized)

- Batch scoring (CSV, JSON, Parquet)

- Real-time inference (data in message queues or REST endpoints)

Loading to Azure ML Datasets

Register cleaned data as an Azure ML Dataset:

```
from azureml.core import Dataset

datastore = ws.get_default_datastore()
dataset = Dataset.Tabular.from_delimited_files(path=(datastore,
'curated/train_data.csv'))
dataset = dataset.register(workspace=ws, name='training-data',
create_new_version=True)
```

This versioned dataset can now be used across multiple experiments, pipelines, and retraining jobs.

Orchestrating End-to-End ETL

ADF Pipelines can be constructed as DAGs (Directed Acyclic Graphs) where each step performs a task:

1. **Extract** from source

2. **Validate** schema

3. **Clean** and transform

4. **Enrich** with AI (optional)

5. **Save** to curated layer

6. **Trigger** model training (optional)

These steps can be monitored and parameterized, allowing the same pipeline to run for different models or environments (dev/test/prod).

Integrating Machine Learning Scoring in ETL

Suppose you want to predict churn probability as part of your ETL process. You can use the **Azure ML Endpoint** in a Web activity inside ADF:

```
{
  "name": "ScoreCustomer",
  "type": "WebActivity",
  "typeProperties": {
    "method": "POST",
    "url": "https://<ml-endpoint>/score",
    "headers": {
      "Authorization": "Bearer <token>",
      "Content-Type": "application/json"
    },
    "body":                           "@{string(concat('{\"data\":',
string(activity('TransformData').output), '}'))}"
  }
}
```

This way, AI models can be applied to streaming or batch data as part of a standard ETL pipeline.

Real-Time ETL with Azure Stream Analytics

For scenarios where low latency is crucial (e.g., fraud detection, telemetry analysis), use **Azure Stream Analytics (ASA)**:

- Ingest from Event Hubs, IoT Hub, or Blob Storage
- Apply windowed transformations (e.g., average, joins, filters)
- Output to Data Lake, SQL DB, Power BI, or Function

Example SQL-like query:

```
SELECT
    deviceId,
    AVG(temperature) AS avg_temp,
    System.Timestamp AS event_time
```

```
INTO curated.sensor_agg
FROM raw.sensor_data TIMESTAMP BY eventTime
GROUP BY deviceId, TumblingWindow(minute, 1)
```

ASA is highly efficient and supports user-defined functions (UDFs) for complex logic.

Testing and Validation

Before promoting a pipeline to production:

- Validate with small sample datasets
- Unit test transformation logic
- Apply schema validation (e.g., using Great Expectations or PyDantic)
- Run backfill tests with historical data
- Create pipeline runbooks for debugging and rollback

Versioning and Lineage

Track versions of:

- Raw and transformed datasets
- ETL scripts and parameters
- Data schema evolution

Tools like Azure Purview or Data Catalog help establish lineage, discoverability, and governance of AI datasets.

Governance and Compliance

- **Access Control**: Use RBAC and data masking where necessary.
- **Audit Logging**: Track all ETL operations for compliance.

- **Data Sensitivity Labels**: Classify datasets as public, confidential, or restricted.

- **GDPR/CCPA Compliance**: Provide traceability of data usage in models.

Best Practices

Area	Best Practice
Transformation	Keep logic modular, testable, and reusable
Schema enforcement	Validate input/output schemas at every ETL stage
Metadata	Tag datasets with description, owner, last updated, and schema
Performance	Use parallel reads, partitioned files, and columnar formats (Parquet/ORC)
Cost optimization	Avoid unnecessary copies, use reserved compute for scheduled jobs
Monitoring	Set up alerting for ETL failures or delays
Automation	Deploy pipelines via CI/CD using ARM or Bicep templates

Summary

ETL pipelines are the arteries that deliver data into the heart of AI systems. By streamlining these pipelines using Azure's rich ecosystem—ADF, Databricks, Synapse, ML pipelines—you can ensure your AI applications are fed with clean, consistent, and timely data. From batch to real-time, from basic transformations to enriched AI scoring, a well-architected ETL pipeline accelerates AI development while reducing operational risk and cost.

In the next section, we will explore how to leverage Azure Stream Analytics for real-time AI workflows—ideal for applications that demand instant insight and automated reactions to events.

Real-Time AI with Azure Stream Analytics

Real-time artificial intelligence (AI) is rapidly transforming how organizations respond to data. Rather than waiting for batch jobs to complete, businesses are increasingly demanding insights and automated actions as events happen. Whether it's monitoring telemetry data from IoT devices, processing live social media streams, or detecting fraud within financial transactions, real-time AI pipelines provide the foundation for smarter, faster decision-making.

Azure Stream Analytics (ASA) is Microsoft's real-time analytics service designed to process streaming data with sub-second latency. It is a fully managed service that integrates seamlessly with Azure's AI and data ecosystem. By combining ASA with Azure Cognitive Services, Azure Machine Learning, and real-time dashboards or alerts, you can build intelligent, scalable, and low-latency AI systems.

This section will cover the architecture, development, integration, and optimization of real-time AI pipelines using Azure Stream Analytics. You'll learn how to set up ASA jobs, process streaming inputs, enrich data with AI services, and output results to dashboards, storage, or even automated triggers.

Core Concepts of Azure Stream Analytics

Azure Stream Analytics is built on a distributed SQL-like query engine that allows you to filter, aggregate, join, and analyze streaming data from various sources. Its key components include:

- **Input**: The data source (Event Hub, IoT Hub, or Blob Storage)

- **Query**: The transformation logic written in ASA's SQL-like language

- **Output**: The data sink (Azure SQL DB, Blob Storage, Power BI, Azure Function, etc.)

- **Functions**: User-Defined Functions (UDFs), Machine Learning integrations, and JavaScript support

Typical Real-Time AI Architecture

A sample architecture for real-time AI could include:

1. **IoT devices or sensors** sending data to Azure IoT Hub or Event Hub.

2. **Azure Stream Analytics job** to process data in-flight.

3. **Azure Cognitive Services or ML models** invoked within the stream query.

4. **Outputs** such as:

    - Real-time dashboards in Power BI

- ○ Storage in Azure Data Lake
- ○ Alerts via Azure Functions or Logic Apps

This pattern supports anomaly detection, image recognition, sentiment analysis, and more in real-time.

Setting Up Azure Stream Analytics

Step 1: Create a Stream Analytics Job

```
az stream-analytics job create \
  --resource-group ai-rg \
  --name realtime-analytics-job \
  --location eastus \
  --output-error-policy Stop
```

Step 2: Define Input Source

Example: Event Hub

```
az stream-analytics input create \
  --job-name realtime-analytics-job \
  --name input-hub \
  --resource-group ai-rg \
  --datasource EventHub \
  --eventhub-namespace mynamespace \
  --eventhub-name telemetry \
  --shared-access-policy-name RootManageSharedAccessKey \
  --consumer-group $Default
```

Step 3: Define Output

Example: Azure SQL Database

```
az stream-analytics output create \
  --job-name realtime-analytics-job \
  --name output-sql \
  --resource-group ai-rg \
  --datasource SqlDatabase \
  --server database-server-name \
  --database-name ai-results \
```

```
--table output_table \
--username myadmin \
--password mypassword
```

Writing Real-Time Queries

ASA queries are based on a familiar SQL-like syntax but are optimized for temporal data.

Example: Average temperature by device every 5 minutes

```
SELECT
  deviceId,
  AVG(temperature) AS avg_temp,
  System.Timestamp AS window_end
INTO
  output-sql
FROM
  input-hub TIMESTAMP BY enqueuedTime
GROUP BY
  deviceId,
  TumblingWindow(minute, 5)
```

ASA supports:

- **Tumbling Windows**: Fixed, non-overlapping intervals
- **Hopping Windows**: Overlapping intervals
- **Sliding Windows**: Based on event times
- **Session Windows**: Dynamic windows based on inactivity

Integrating AI with ASA

1. Azure Machine Learning Integration

You can call an Azure ML endpoint directly from ASA using the `AzureML` function.

```
SELECT
  deviceId,
```

```
  temperature,
  AzureML.PredictChurn(temperature, humidity) AS churn_score
INTO
  output-sql
FROM
  input-hub
```

To enable this, register the ML endpoint in the ASA job configuration. The endpoint must be a REST interface accepting JSON and returning a prediction.

2. Calling REST APIs with JavaScript UDFs

ASA allows custom JavaScript UDFs to call Cognitive Services or other APIs.

Create a JavaScript function like this:

```
function sentimentScore(text) {
    var request = require('request');
    var options = {
        url:
'https://<region>.api.cognitive.microsoft.com/text/analytics/v3.0/se
ntiment',
        headers: { 'Ocp-Apim-Subscription-Key': '<api-key>' },
        method: 'POST',
        body: JSON.stringify({ "documents": [{ "language": "en",
"id": "1", "text": text }] })
    };

    var score = 0.0;
    request(options, function (error, response, body) {
        if (!error && response.statusCode == 200) {
            var result = JSON.parse(body);
            score = result.documents[0].confidenceScores.positive;
        }
    });

    return score;
}
```

Then call it in your query:

```
SELECT
```

```
  deviceId,
  sentimentScore(feedback) AS sentiment
INTO
  output-sql
FROM
  input-hub
```

Real-Time Dashboards

One of the most powerful features of ASA is native **Power BI output integration**.

To stream data to a Power BI dashboard:

1. Authorize ASA to access Power BI workspace
2. Create a streaming dataset
3. Output from ASA using PowerBI output
4. Build visualizations on live data

This is ideal for:

- Monitoring customer sentiment
- Tracking real-time stock performance
- Visualizing IoT telemetry

Event-Driven Automation

Combine ASA with **Azure Functions** or **Logic Apps** to act on data.

Example:

```
SELECT *
INTO alert-function
FROM input-hub
WHERE temperature > 80 AND vibration > 20
```

The `alert-function` output triggers an Azure Function that sends an email, shuts down a device, or writes to a ticketing system.

You can even pipe this into **Azure Synapse Link** for downstream analytics.

Performance and Scaling

ASA is designed for high throughput with low latency. Optimize performance with:

- **Partitioned inputs**: Use `PARTITION BY` for parallelism
- **Stream units (SUs)**: Scale up via Azure Portal or CLI
- **Compact output schema**: Minimize size of records
- **Avoid blocking queries**: Use windows wisely

Monitor job metrics like:

- Input rate (events/sec)
- Output rate
- Late events
- Backlogged data

Security and Access Control

- Use **managed identities** to authenticate with secure outputs
- Limit public access to ML endpoints and use **private endpoints**
- Encrypt data in transit and at rest
- Use **Azure Policy** to enforce secure ASA configurations

Cost Considerations

ASA charges are based on:

- Stream Units (compute resource)
- Number of inputs and outputs
- Complexity of the query

Tips to reduce cost:

- Minimize number of SU by simplifying logic
- Use **batch outputs** instead of frequent small writes
- Stop jobs when not in use
- Use **reservations** for long-running jobs

Real-World Scenarios

Scenario	Use Case
Smart Manufacturing	Detect equipment failure from telemetry
Live Sports and Betting	Real-time odds adjustment and player tracking
Fraud Detection	Flag suspicious transactions as they occur
Customer Support Dashboards	Monitor call sentiment in real-time
Social Media Monitoring	Track and respond to brand mentions instantly
Retail	Detect in-store movement patterns and trigger promotions

---

Best Practices

Practice	Recommendation
Time Management	Always specify `TIMESTAMP BY` for proper event time tracking

Late Arrival Handling	Define `LateArrivalMaxDelay` to buffer delayed events
Replayability	Store input in Event Hub Capture or Blob to reprocess on failure
Reusability	Modularize with views and reuse across jobs
AI Integration	Keep scoring fast; use lightweight models or batch external calls
Monitoring	Set up alerts on latency, dropped events, or error rates

Summary

Real-time AI applications are no longer a futuristic concept—they are essential for competitive, responsive, and intelligent systems across industries. With Azure Stream Analytics, developers can build powerful real-time processing pipelines that integrate seamlessly with Azure's AI services, scale elastically, and respond to data as it arrives.

By combining streaming data with dynamic queries, real-time dashboards, and AI enrichment, Azure enables you to automate decisions and unlock insights that were previously out of reach. In the next section, we'll focus on securing these pipelines and the sensitive data that flows through them—ensuring your AI systems remain trustworthy, compliant, and resilient.

Securing Data Pipelines

Security is a foundational pillar of any enterprise data architecture, particularly when dealing with AI systems that rely on vast volumes of sensitive, diverse, and often proprietary data. Data pipelines—responsible for ingesting, transforming, and delivering this data—must be carefully secured to prevent data breaches, ensure compliance with regulatory standards, and maintain trustworthiness in AI outcomes. Whether data is at rest, in motion, or in use, security must be enforced at every stage of the pipeline lifecycle.

This section outlines a comprehensive approach to securing data pipelines within the Azure ecosystem. It covers identity and access management, network security, data encryption, secret management, auditing, and best practices to ensure the confidentiality, integrity, and availability of data as it moves through AI systems.

Understanding the Attack Surface

Data pipelines involve multiple services and components, which increases the attack surface:

- **Storage**: Data Lake, Blob Storage, SQL, Cosmos DB

- **Compute**: Azure Data Factory, Databricks, Functions, Stream Analytics
- **AI Services**: Cognitive Services, Azure Machine Learning endpoints
- **Integration points**: APIs, webhooks, external connectors

Potential threats include:

- Unauthorized access or privilege escalation
- Data exfiltration or leakage
- Injection or tampering in transformation logic
- Exposure of API keys or secrets
- Insufficient audit logging

Securing a pipeline requires coordinated policies, tools, and practices.

Identity and Access Management (IAM)

Azure provides fine-grained role-based access control (RBAC) to manage access to resources.

RBAC Best Practices

- Follow the **principle of least privilege**—assign only the permissions a user or service requires.
- Use **built-in roles** such as:
  - Reader
  - Contributor
  - Storage Blob Data Contributor
  - AzureML Data Scientist
- Create **custom roles** for specific tasks when needed.
- Use **Azure Active Directory (AAD)** groups to manage access at scale.

Managed Identities

Use **managed identities** for services like Data Factory, Functions, and Databricks to authenticate securely without storing credentials.

Example: Grant Data Factory access to a storage account

```
az role assignment create \
  --assignee-object-id <data-factory-managed-identity-id> \
  --role "Storage Blob Data Contributor" \
  --scope                                      /subscriptions/<sub-
id>/resourceGroups/<rg>/providers/Microsoft.Storage/storageAccounts/
<storage-account>
```

Network Security

Restricting network access prevents unauthorized entry into your pipeline infrastructure.

Virtual Networks (VNets)

- **Integrate key services into VNets,** including:

  - Azure Data Factory Integration Runtime

  - Azure Databricks Workspaces

  - Azure Machine Learning Compute

- Use **Private Endpoints** to access services like Blob Storage, Data Lake, or SQL without exposing them to the internet.

Network Rules

- Enable **firewall rules** on storage accounts and databases.

- Whitelist only necessary IPs or VNets.

- Deny all by default (`networkRuleSet.defaultAction` = Deny).

Example: Restrict access to a Data Lake account

```
az storage account network-rule add \
  --resource-group ai-rg \
  --account-name mydatalake \
```

```
--vnet-name ai-vnet \
--subnet default
```

Data Encryption

Data must be encrypted both **at rest** and **in transit**.

At Rest

- All Azure storage services encrypt data at rest using **Microsoft-managed keys** by default.

- Use **customer-managed keys (CMK)** in Azure Key Vault for enhanced control.

- Enable **soft delete** and **immutability policies** to protect against accidental deletion or ransomware attacks.

Example: Enable CMK on Blob Storage

```
az storage account update \
  --name myaccount \
  --resource-group ai-rg \
  --encryption-key-source Microsoft.Keyvault \
  --keyvault-encryption-key-url <key-url>
```

In Transit

- Use **HTTPS** for all API calls and storage access.

- Enforce TLS 1.2 or higher.

- Disable public HTTP endpoints.

Secret Management

Avoid hardcoding secrets like API keys, credentials, or connection strings.

Use Azure Key Vault

Azure Key Vault stores secrets, certificates, and encryption keys securely.

- Integrate with Data Factory, Azure ML, Functions, and other services.

- Access secrets via managed identity authentication.

Example: Retrieve secret in Python

```python
from azure.identity import DefaultAzureCredential
from azure.keyvault.secrets import SecretClient

credential = DefaultAzureCredential()
client = SecretClient(vault_url="https://myvault.vault.azure.net/",
credential=credential)
secret = client.get_secret("my-db-password")
```

Key Vault also supports access policies, logging, and RBAC integration.

Auditing and Monitoring

Monitoring is critical for detecting and responding to security incidents.

Azure Monitor

Track and alert on:

- Unauthorized access attempts

- Unusual volume of requests

- Errors or failures in pipeline stages

Diagnostic Logs

Enable diagnostic logs for:

- Storage accounts

- Data Factory

- Key Vault

- SQL Database

Log Analytics

Query and analyze logs using Kusto Query Language (KQL):

```
AzureDiagnostics
| where ResourceType == "STORAGEACCOUNTS"
| where OperationName == "GetBlob"
| summarize count() by CallerIPAddress, Resource, bin(TimeGenerated,
1h)
```

Data Classification and Labeling

Label data according to its sensitivity:

- Public

- Internal

- Confidential

- Highly   confidential

Use **Azure Purview** to:

- Scan   and   catalog   datasets

- Classify   data   using   built-in   or   custom   rules

- Track   lineage   and   usage   of   data   across   pipelines

Purview integrates with Microsoft Information Protection (MIP) for end-to-end governance.

Compliance and Regulatory Standards

Azure provides compliance certifications for HIPAA, GDPR, ISO 27001, SOC, FedRAMP, and more.

Ensure your pipelines adhere to:

- **Data   minimization**:   Collect   only   necessary   data.

- **Data residency**: Store and process data in allowed geographic regions.

- **Data retention**: Implement lifecycle management policies.
- **Consent and transparency**: Track data usage for auditability.

Secure DevOps for Data Pipelines

Incorporate security into the CI/CD lifecycle of your data workflows.

- Use **Infrastructure as Code (IaC)** with Bicep, ARM, or Terraform.
- Scan IaC templates for misconfigurations using tools like **Checkov** or **tflint**.
- Enforce **code review and approvals** in GitHub Actions or Azure DevOps.
- Automate **security testing** and **policy checks** before deploying.

Example GitHub Action to check for secrets in code:

```
- name: Check for exposed secrets
  uses: zricethezav/gitleaks-action@v1.5.0
```

Best Practices Checklist

Area	Recommendation
Authentication	Use AAD and managed identities, not connection strings
Authorization	Apply least privilege with RBAC
Data Access	Use VNet + Private Link to secure storage and compute
Encryption	Enable CMK and enforce HTTPS/TLS 1.2
Secrets	Store in Azure Key Vault; never hardcode credentials
Monitoring	Enable diagnostic logs and alerts for anomalous activity
Data Classification	Use Azure Purview for sensitivity tagging and data lineage

Compliance	Align with industry and regional data protection regulations

Summary

Securing your AI data pipelines is not optional—it's a fundamental requirement for building trustworthy, compliant, and production-ready systems. Azure provides a comprehensive toolset to secure every aspect of your data journey, from access control and network isolation to encryption, secret management, and monitoring.

By combining strong identity policies, secure network design, rigorous encryption, and vigilant monitoring, you can build pipelines that not only support innovative AI capabilities but do so with resilience and integrity. In the next chapter, we'll explore ethical considerations and responsible AI practices that ensure your systems remain aligned with societal values and legal obligations.

Chapter 7: Ethics, Compliance, and Responsible AI

Understanding AI Ethics and Governance

As artificial intelligence becomes an integral part of business and society, the need for ethical, transparent, and accountable AI systems has grown increasingly urgent. While AI can unlock powerful benefits—ranging from improved healthcare to more efficient logistics—it also introduces significant ethical challenges such as bias, discrimination, lack of transparency, privacy concerns, and potential for misuse. These challenges are amplified in enterprise settings, where AI decisions can affect customers, employees, and entire communities.

This section explores the foundations of AI ethics, the key principles of responsible AI development, and the governance frameworks needed to operationalize ethical AI practices within Azure-based solutions. We'll look at real-world examples, common pitfalls, and how Microsoft Azure supports responsible AI through tooling, transparency, policy integration, and organizational alignment.

What Is AI Ethics?

AI ethics is a multidisciplinary field that addresses how to design, develop, deploy, and govern AI systems in ways that are just, fair, and beneficial to society. It blends considerations from technology, philosophy, law, and social science.

Core ethical concerns in AI include:

- **Bias and fairness**: Avoiding discriminatory outcomes against individuals or groups.

- **Transparency**: Making AI decisions and logic understandable to users and stakeholders.

- **Accountability**: Assigning responsibility when AI systems go wrong.

- **Privacy**: Protecting sensitive data and respecting user consent.

- **Safety and robustness**: Ensuring AI behaves reliably in all scenarios.

- **Human autonomy**: Preserving human control over critical decisions.

These principles must be baked into every stage of AI development—from ideation to deployment and monitoring.

Why Governance Is Critical

AI governance refers to the policies, procedures, roles, and oversight mechanisms that guide the ethical use of AI within an organization. Without governance, even well-meaning AI initiatives can cause harm due to blind spots, lack of documentation, or insufficient testing.

Good AI governance:

- Prevents reputational and legal risks.

- Aligns AI outcomes with organizational values.

- Encourages collaboration across data scientists, legal, compliance, and executive teams.

- Builds public trust in AI-powered products and services.

Azure enables governance through a combination of compliance tooling, data access controls, responsible AI dashboards, and integration with enterprise IT and audit systems.

Principles of Responsible AI (Microsoft's Framework)

Microsoft has articulated six core principles that guide its responsible AI efforts. These principles can serve as a blueprint for any Azure-based AI project:

1. **Fairness**
   AI systems should treat all people fairly and avoid discrimination. *Example*: An AI hiring system should not disadvantage applicants based on gender or ethnicity.

2. **Reliability and Safety**
   AI systems should operate reliably and safely, even under unexpected conditions. *Example*: A self-driving model should handle edge cases like pedestrians on unmarked roads.

3. **Privacy and Security**
   AI systems must safeguard personal data and maintain confidentiality. *Example*: Healthcare ML models should follow HIPAA and GDPR requirements.

4. **Inclusiveness**
   AI should empower everyone and reflect diverse needs. *Example*: Voice recognition systems must understand various accents and speech patterns.

5. **Transparency**
   AI systems should provide insight into how they work and why they make certain decisions.
   Example: A financial model should log and expose factors leading to credit rejections.

6. **Accountability**
   People must be accountable for AI systems and their impacts.
   Example: Audit trails should be available for regulatory inspection or customer complaints.

Real-World Ethical Risks in AI

Ethical failures in AI are not hypothetical—they have occurred across industries:

- **COMPAS**: A criminal justice algorithm found to be racially biased.

- **Amazon's Resume AI**: Discontinued after it discriminated against female applicants.

- **Facial Recognition**: Misidentification and surveillance concerns raised by civil rights groups.

These examples highlight the importance of not just focusing on model accuracy but also ensuring fairness, transparency, and social impact.

Building Ethical AI Pipelines in Azure

To operationalize ethics, organizations must implement tools, policies, and reviews throughout the AI lifecycle.

1. Problem Framing

- Define the AI use case and intended users.

- Identify potential harms and stakeholders.

- Document assumptions, goals, and constraints.

2. Data Collection

- Ensure datasets are representative and unbiased.

- Avoid proxies for protected characteristics (e.g., ZIP code as proxy for race).
- Apply differential privacy techniques where necessary.

3. Model Training

- Use fairness-aware algorithms (e.g., reweighing, adversarial debiasing).
- Include multiple evaluation metrics (accuracy, F1, disparate impact).
- Log all versions and hyperparameters for reproducibility.

4. Validation

- Conduct bias audits and ethical red-teaming.
- Include diverse test groups.
- Validate interpretability using SHAP or LIME.

5. Deployment

- Include fallback mechanisms (human-in-the-loop).
- Expose model logic and metrics where appropriate.
- Monitor for model drift and unintended consequences.

6. Monitoring

- Log all inference requests and outcomes.
- Track usage patterns and flag anomalies.
- Collect user feedback and complaints.

Azure Tools for Responsible AI

Microsoft provides native tools and integrations for responsible AI:

Tool	Purpose

Azure ML Fairness Dashboard	Assess disparity across groups
InterpretML	Explain model predictions using SHAP, LIME
Azure Responsible AI Dashboard	Visualize and assess fairness, error, causality
Data Privacy Toolkit	Apply anonymization, masking, and compliance utilities
Model Data Collector	Collect inputs and outputs for audit logging
Azure Policy	Enforce security and compliance on AI resources
GitHub Actions / DevOps Pipelines	Automate testing and deployment with built-in guardrails

These tools help integrate responsible AI principles into the daily workflows of data science and engineering teams.

Organizational Practices for Ethical AI

Tools alone aren't enough—ethics must be embedded into the organizational culture.

- **Establish AI ethics committees** or review boards.
- **Train teams** on AI risks and responsible practices.
- **Include ethics checkpoints** in model development lifecycle.
- **Create escalation paths** for whistleblowing or ethical concerns.
- **Engage stakeholders** early and frequently, especially those impacted by AI.

Documentation templates, checklists, and open Q&A forums can also reinforce ethical vigilance.

Regulatory Considerations

As governments catch up with AI, organizations must stay informed and compliant:

- **EU AI Act**: Requires classification and registration of high-risk AI systems.

- **GDPR**: Regulates automated decision-making and requires explainability.

- **HIPAA**: Applies to health-related AI in the U.S.

- **CCPA**: California's consumer data protection law impacts AI models trained on personal data.

- **Algorithmic Accountability Act (proposed)**: Aims to mandate impact assessments.

Using Azure's policy framework, you can enforce geography-based data residency, restrict access, and document consent where required.

Case Study: Ethical AI in Financial Services

A multinational bank used Azure Machine Learning to build a credit scoring model. To ensure ethical practices:

- They used **Azure Fairness Dashboard** to evaluate model bias across gender, ethnicity, and age.

- **SHAP values** explained why certain applicants were denied credit.

- The model was deployed with **confidence thresholds** and flagged borderline scores for human review.

- An **ethics review committee** signed off before production deployment.

This resulted in a fairer, more transparent model that passed regulatory inspection and improved public trust.

Summary

Ethics in AI is not a constraint—it's a strategic advantage. It leads to safer systems, increased trust, fewer legal and reputational risks, and more inclusive outcomes. By adopting ethical principles, governance structures, and technical safeguards, organizations can ensure that AI works for everyone, not just a privileged few.

Azure provides the frameworks, tools, and integrations to embed responsible AI into every stage of development and deployment. In the next section, we'll explore how to leverage these tools in practice, using Azure's built-in services for fairness, explainability, and privacy preservation.

Azure Tools for Responsible AI (Fairness, Explainability, Privacy)

Microsoft Azure offers a comprehensive set of tools and frameworks that help organizations build AI systems aligned with ethical principles and regulatory compliance. These tools support key pillars of responsible AI—**fairness, explainability**, and **privacy**—which are essential for earning trust, avoiding bias, and enabling auditability. This section explores Azure's capabilities for addressing each of these areas in depth, with practical guidance on implementation and integration into real-world AI workflows.

These tools are not only designed for compliance, but to empower developers, data scientists, and business stakeholders to proactively evaluate, understand, and improve AI systems.

Fairness: Detecting and Mitigating Bias

Bias in AI systems often stems from imbalanced data, flawed assumptions, or inadequate testing. Azure helps detect and mitigate these risks using toolkits that evaluate performance across different subgroups and support model corrections.

Azure Machine Learning Fairness Dashboard

The Fairness Dashboard, part of Azure Machine Learning's Responsible AI toolset, enables practitioners to:

- Assess how model predictions vary across groups (e.g., age, race, gender)

- Visualize performance metrics like accuracy, precision, recall per subgroup

- Simulate "what if" scenarios to observe the impact of input feature changes

Example Workflow

1. **Train your model** and log the run in Azure ML.

2. **Capture predictions**, true labels, and sensitive feature columns.

3. **Load** the dashboard:

```
from raiwidgets import FairnessDashboard
from fairlearn.metrics import MetricFrame, selection_rate,
accuracy_score

FairnessDashboard(
```

```
    sensitive_features=sensitive_features,
    y_true=labels,
    y_pred=model_predictions
)
```

4. Use the visual UI to inspect disparities and identify sources of unfair outcomes.

Fairlearn Integration

Azure ML integrates with the Fairlearn package, allowing you to calculate and mitigate unfair treatment in models:

```
from      fairlearn.reductions      import      ExponentiatedGradient,
DemographicParity

mitigator      =      ExponentiatedGradient(estimator=model,
constraints=DemographicParity())
mitigator.fit(X_train,                                    y_train,
sensitive_features=sensitive_features)
predictions = mitigator.predict(X_test)
```

Fairlearn supports various fairness constraints and includes metrics like:

- Demographic parity difference

- Equal opportunity difference

- False positive/negative rate parity

These tools enable not just detection, but iterative improvement of model fairness.

Explainability: Making AI Transparent

Explainability is critical for building trust in AI systems. Stakeholders—especially in regulated industries—need to understand why a model made a particular decision. Azure provides multiple ways to make models interpretable:

InterpretML and Responsible AI Dashboard

InterpretML is a Microsoft library that enables local and global explanation of model behavior using methods like:

- **SHAP (SHapley Additive Explanations)**: Feature contribution scores

- **LIME (Local Interpretable Model-agnostic Explanations)**: Perturbation-based analysis

- **EBM (Explainable Boosting Machines)**: Interpretable generalized additive models

```
from interpret.blackbox import TabularExplainer
from raiwidgets import ExplanationDashboard

explainer = TabularExplainer(model, X_train)
global_explanation = explainer.explain_global(X_test)

ExplanationDashboard(global_explanation, X_test)
```

The Responsible AI Dashboard combines multiple tools into a single, interactive interface that includes:

- Fairness   analysis

- Error   analysis

- Model   performance

- Causal   inference

- Counterfactual   explanations

It supports models trained in scikit-learn, LightGBM, XGBoost, PyTorch, TensorFlow, and AutoML pipelines.

SHAP Visualizations

SHAP plots can be generated to show the influence of each feature:

```
import shap

explainer = shap.Explainer(model.predict, X_train)
shap_values = explainer(X_test)

shap.plots.waterfall(shap_values[0])
```

These plots are invaluable for regulatory reports, customer inquiries, and model debugging.

Privacy: Protecting Sensitive Information

Protecting user privacy is both a legal obligation and a moral imperative. Azure supports privacy-aware AI development through data anonymization, differential privacy, access controls, and compliance tooling.

Data Anonymization and Masking

Before training or sharing datasets, sensitive fields can be masked or tokenized using Azure services or open-source tools.

Example anonymization techniques:

- Redact or hash personally identifiable information (PII)
- Use pseudonyms for names and IDs
- Bucket ages or incomes into ranges

Azure Purview (data governance) can classify and identify sensitive fields based on built-in or custom policies.

Differential Privacy

Differential privacy adds statistical noise to data or outputs, making it hard to infer individual records from aggregate data.

Microsoft provides tools like **WhiteNoise** (now integrated into OpenDP) to apply differential privacy in model training and evaluation.

Use cases include:

- Sharing insights without leaking individual data
- Training models on synthetic datasets
- Building privacy-respecting recommendation systems

Role-Based Access Control (RBAC)

Azure enforces RBAC on:

- Data sources (Blob, SQL, Cosmos)
- ML models and endpoints

- Key   Vault   secrets

- Pipelines   and   compute   clusters

Define roles such as:

- Reader   (view-only)

- Contributor   (edit)

- Owner   (manage   access)

- Custom   roles   with   limited   scope   (e.g.,   "Model   Evaluator")

Private Links and Network Isolation

Sensitive model endpoints and storage accounts should be accessed only over secure networks:

- Enable **Private Endpoints** to prevent public internet access.

- Restrict Azure Functions or Data Factory to trusted VNets.

- Use **Service Endpoints** for traffic routing.

Responsible AI Integration in CI/CD Pipelines

You can integrate fairness, explainability, and privacy checks into your DevOps pipelines:

Example: Azure DevOps Pipeline

```
- task: UsePythonVersion@0
  inputs:
    versionSpec: '3.9'

- script: |
    pip install azureml-sdk fairlearn interpret raiwidgets
    python run_fairness_check.py
  displayName: 'Run Responsible AI Checks'
```

This script could:

- Load the latest model and test dataset
- Calculate fairness metrics
- Generate SHAP visualizations
- Export a PDF report
- Fail the build if thresholds are exceeded

This ensures every new model version is vetted for responsible practices.

Visualizing Responsible AI Metrics in Azure ML Studio

Once a model is registered and scored, you can access explainability and fairness dashboards from within Azure Machine Learning Studio.

- Navigate to the **Registered Model**
- Click on **Responsible AI**
- Select **Fairness**, **Interpretability**, or **Error Analysis**
- Filter by sensitive features or use subpopulation slices

Azure ML tracks lineage from dataset to model to endpoint—supporting auditability and reproducibility.

Enterprise Use Case: Healthcare AI

A hospital network uses Azure ML to predict readmission risk. To ensure fairness and privacy:

- Sensitive attributes (age, gender, race) are tagged in the dataset.
- Fairlearn is used to ensure equal opportunity across patient demographics.
- SHAP explanations help clinicians understand the top contributors (e.g., number of ER visits, medication changes).
- Azure Key Vault secures API keys and model access tokens.
- Role-based access is enforced so only licensed staff can access predictions.

The system is compliant with HIPAA and local data protection laws while maintaining high accuracy and interpretability.

Summary

Responsible AI requires a combination of ethical principles, governance policies, and technical tools. Azure delivers a mature ecosystem to support fairness, explainability, and privacy through both open-source libraries and integrated platform services.

By embedding these capabilities into your AI development lifecycle—from data ingestion to model deployment—you can ensure your solutions are not only effective but ethical, transparent, and trustworthy.

The next section will address the legal and regulatory landscape surrounding AI, providing guidance on how to align your Azure AI systems with local and international compliance frameworks.

Legal and Regulatory Considerations

As artificial intelligence systems become more widespread and influential, regulators around the world are responding with new laws and frameworks aimed at ensuring that AI technologies are used safely, ethically, and responsibly. For developers and organizations building AI systems on Azure, understanding and adhering to these legal and regulatory requirements is essential—not only to avoid penalties and reputational damage but also to build trust with users and stakeholders.

This section provides a deep dive into the current legal landscape surrounding AI, with a focus on key international regulations, compliance strategies, and how Azure's ecosystem enables organizations to meet these standards. It also outlines best practices for implementing governance controls that align with both local laws and global ethical guidelines.

Why Regulation Matters in AI

Unlike traditional software, AI systems introduce novel risks:

- **Automated decision-making** may affect access to employment, healthcare, or credit.

- **Opaque models** make accountability difficult in case of harm.

- **Bias and discrimination** can become embedded in predictive systems.

- **Mass data collection** may violate privacy laws.

- **Cybersecurity risks** grow as models become more powerful and data-intensive.

Laws and regulations aim to ensure AI is developed and deployed in ways that protect human rights, ensure fairness, and preserve privacy and safety. Organizations must prepare for a future where **AI compliance is mandatory**, not optional.

Key Global and Regional Regulations

General Data Protection Regulation (GDPR) – EU

One of the most influential data protection laws globally, the GDPR impacts any organization processing the personal data of EU citizens.

Relevant AI provisions:

- **Article 22**: Right not to be subject to automated decision-making.
- **Recital 71**: Requires meaningful information about the logic involved.
- **Data minimization** and **purpose limitation** must be enforced.
- Consent must be **freely given**, **specific**, and **informed**.

Azure Strategies:

- Use **Azure Purview** to classify and govern personal data.
- Enforce access controls with **Azure RBAC** and **Key Vault**.
- Use **Responsible AI Dashboard** to explain decision logic.
- Apply **data anonymization or differential privacy** to protect user identity.

EU Artificial Intelligence Act (AIA) – Proposed

This upcoming legislation introduces a risk-based regulatory framework for AI systems.

AI Risk Tiers:

- **Unacceptable risk**: Prohibited (e.g., social scoring, subliminal manipulation)
- **High risk**: Subject to strict requirements (e.g., biometric identification, credit scoring)

- **Limited risk**: Transparency obligations (e.g., chatbots)
- **Minimal risk**: No additional legal obligations

Compliance for High-Risk AI:

- Maintain documentation and audit logs
- Conduct conformity assessments
- Ensure robustness, accuracy, and cybersecurity
- Enable human oversight

Azure Tools for Compliance:

- Use **Azure Machine Learning Lineage** to track data, models, and decisions
- Store compliance reports in **Azure Blob Storage** with immutability settings
- Audit workflows using **Azure Monitor** and **Log Analytics**

HIPAA – U.S. Healthcare

The Health Insurance Portability and Accountability Act (HIPAA) governs health-related data in the U.S.

AI Implications:

- Any machine learning model using **Protected Health Information (PHI)** must comply.
- AI systems that support diagnosis, treatment, or patient communication must meet security and privacy standards.

Azure Compliance Capabilities:

- **Azure Security Center** and **Compliance Manager** provide HIPAA templates.
- Use **Azure Policy** to enforce resource configurations.
- Store PHI in **HIPAA-compliant services** like Azure SQL with Transparent Data Encryption (TDE).

- Implement **Business Associate Agreements (BAAs)** for third-party processors.

CCPA & CPRA – California Privacy Laws

California Consumer Privacy Act (CCPA) and its amendment, California Privacy Rights Act (CPRA), empower users to control how their data is used.

Key Provisions:

- Right to know what personal data is collected
- Right to delete personal data
- Right to opt out of data sale or sharing
- Right to access meaningful information about automated decision-making

Azure Recommendations:

- Log user consent in **Azure Cosmos DB** or similar
- Track personal data flows using **Azure Purview**
- Provide opt-out capabilities via **API endpoints** or **Azure App Service**

Algorithmic Accountability Act – U.S. (Proposed)

Would require companies to perform **impact assessments** on automated decision systems, especially when used in critical domains like employment, education, or housing.

Azure Readiness:

- Use **Responsible AI Scorecards** to document performance and fairness
- Enable internal review boards or governance workflows via **Power Automate**
- Maintain evidence in **Azure DevOps** repositories for audit

---

Implementing Legal Controls in Azure

1. Data Sovereignty and Residency

Ensure that data is stored and processed in approved geographic locations.

- Select appropriate Azure regions when creating storage accounts.

- Use **Azure** **Policy** to enforce region restrictions.

2. Data Access and Logging

Enable detailed access logs to track who accessed what data and when.

```
az storage logging update \
  --account-name mystorage \
  --log rwd \
  --retention 30 \
  --services b
```

Enable **Storage Analytics Logging** or integrate with **Microsoft Sentinel** for SOC reporting.

3. Consent Management

Log and enforce user consent for data usage, especially for AI inference.

Example architecture:

- Consent captured via frontend app

- Stored securely in **Azure** **Table** **Storage**

- Checked before each prediction request is fulfilled

Governance Frameworks

To streamline compliance, many organizations adopt AI-specific governance models.

Components:

- **Policy** **Frameworks**: Data handling, consent, model review

- **Ethics** **Boards**: Review AI projects from a societal and legal perspective

- **Audit** **Trails**: Immutable logs of decisions and model versions

- **Model Cards and Datasheets**: Structured documentation templates for transparency

Azure's ecosystem supports these through:

- **Azure ML Model Registry** with metadata
- **GitHub** or **Azure DevOps** for code and documentation versioning
- **Logic Apps** to automate compliance workflows

Documentation and Reporting

Maintain detailed records of:

- Training data provenance
- Evaluation metrics and fairness results
- Model architecture and hyperparameters
- Risk assessments and stakeholder sign-offs

Azure ML lets you attach metadata and documents to models, which helps during audits and regulatory inspections.

Future Regulatory Trends

AI regulation is accelerating globally:

- **Brazil's LGPD** includes AI provisions aligned with GDPR
- **China's AI Guidelines** emphasize security, national interest, and ethics
- **OECD and UNESCO** have released non-binding AI principles
- National and regional **AI sandboxes** are emerging to test new policies

Azure's global compliance portfolio helps multinational organizations adapt to this evolving landscape.

Best Practices Checklist

Area	Best Practice
Data Privacy	Use anonymization, masking, and role-based access controls
Documentation	Maintain data sheets, model cards, and fairness evaluations
Compliance Automation	Implement policies via Azure Policy, CI/CD pipelines, and alerts
Consent and Transparency	Track and respect user preferences for automated decisions
Audit Logs	Enable system-level and application-level logging
Geographic Residency	Ensure data is stored in legally permitted regions
Security	Encrypt data in transit and at rest; enforce private network paths

Summary

Legal and regulatory compliance is no longer a "checkbox" activity—it must be embedded into every layer of AI development and deployment. With evolving global frameworks like the EU AI Act, HIPAA, GDPR, and state-level privacy laws, AI solutions on Azure must be designed from the ground up to meet these standards.

Fortunately, Azure provides a comprehensive set of services, policies, and governance tools that empower organizations to build compliant, secure, and ethically sound AI systems. By staying proactive and informed, developers and decision-makers can create intelligent applications that are not only effective, but also accountable, inclusive, and legally defensible.

Chapter 8: Real-World Use Cases and Deployment Strategies

Case Study: Smart Healthcare

The healthcare industry is undergoing a significant digital transformation driven by the integration of artificial intelligence (AI) into clinical and operational workflows. AI in healthcare promises to improve diagnosis, personalize treatment, reduce administrative burdens, and enhance patient engagement. In this case study, we explore how a healthcare organization leverages Microsoft Azure's AI and cloud infrastructure to build, deploy, and scale an intelligent healthcare system that augments human expertise and improves patient outcomes.

This section provides a comprehensive walkthrough of the design, implementation, and deployment of an AI-powered healthcare solution on Azure. We will focus on practical applications including medical imaging analysis, predictive analytics, patient monitoring, and virtual care, as well as the compliance and security considerations necessary in a highly regulated domain.

Background and Objectives

A national healthcare provider with a network of hospitals and clinics wants to build an AI-driven platform to assist radiologists in diagnosing lung conditions from chest X-rays. The goals are:

- Accelerate diagnosis by providing AI-based second opinions.

- Prioritize urgent cases using predictive scoring.

- Reduce radiologist workload through automation.

- Ensure HIPAA and GDPR compliance.

- Deploy the solution across multiple clinical sites.

The provider chooses Azure for its scalability, built-in compliance support, and rich ecosystem of AI and healthcare-specific tools.

Architecture Overview

The architecture integrates several Azure components in a modular, secure, and scalable design:

- **Azure Blob Storage**: Stores incoming medical images (DICOM format).

- **Azure Data Factory**: Orchestrates ingestion from PACS (Picture Archiving and Communication System).

- **Azure Machine Learning**: Hosts and manages the diagnostic model.

- **Azure Functions**: Processes events (e.g., new image uploaded) and routes to ML scoring.

- **Azure App Service / API Management**: Exposes AI inference results to internal apps.

- **Power BI / Power Apps**: For visualization and clinician feedback.

- **Azure Monitor / Log Analytics**: Tracks usage and performance.

- **Azure Key Vault**: Secures API keys and connection strings.

All services are contained within a **VNet** with **private endpoints**, and **RBAC** is enforced across services.

AI Model Development

The team collects and anonymizes a dataset of over 50,000 chest X-ray images labeled by certified radiologists. The dataset includes metadata such as age, gender, symptoms, and diagnosis outcomes.

Preprocessing and Labeling

- Convert DICOM images to PNG/JPEG for visualization.

- Apply histogram equalization and resizing for consistency.

- Use Azure Data Lake to store raw and processed images.

```python
import pydicom
from PIL import Image

def dicom_to_jpeg(dicom_path, output_path):
    ds = pydicom.dcmread(dicom_path)
    img = ds.pixel_array
    img = Image.fromarray(img)
    img.save(output_path)
```

Model Architecture

The AI model uses a **ResNet-50 CNN** pretrained on ImageNet and fine-tuned on the healthcare dataset. The model outputs:

- Probability scores for pneumonia, COVID-19, tuberculosis, and other lung conditions.

- Confidence   intervals.

- Localization   heatmaps   for   abnormal   regions   (Grad-CAM).

Training and Evaluation

Training is done using **Azure ML Compute Clusters** with GPU nodes. Evaluation metrics include:

- Accuracy: 91.4%

- AUC   (Pneumonia):   0.96

- False   negatives   are   manually   reviewed.

Responsible AI Integration

- Fairness   checks   are   performed   using   **Fairlearn**   across   age   and   gender.

- SHAP   values   are   used   for   explainability.

- A   **Responsible   AI   dashboard**   is   generated   for   internal   auditing.

Deployment with Azure ML

The trained model is registered and deployed as a REST endpoint:

```
from azureml.core.webservice import AciWebservice, Webservice

deployment_config = AciWebservice.deploy_configuration(cpu_cores=2,
memory_gb=4)
service = Model.deploy(workspace=ws,
                    name='xray-diagnosis-service',
                    models=[model],
```

```
                inference_config=inference_config,
                deployment_config=deployment_config)
service.wait_for_deployment(show_output=True)
```

For production, the model is deployed to **Azure Kubernetes Service (AKS)** with autoscaling enabled.

Integration with Clinical Systems

Event-Driven Scoring

Azure Functions monitor Blob Storage for new X-ray images:

```
import azure.functions as func

def main(myblob: func.InputStream):
    image_data = myblob.read()
    result = call_ml_endpoint(image_data)
    store_result(result)
```

Results are stored in a secure database and surfaced through a clinician-facing dashboard built in Power BI and integrated with Microsoft Teams.

Decision Support

The AI system provides:

- A list of top three probable diagnoses.

- A severity score (0–100) to prioritize review.

- Visual overlays indicating affected lung regions.

The clinician uses this to verify or overrule the AI prediction, improving trust and transparency.

Compliance and Privacy

All components comply with **HIPAA**, **GDPR**, and **local health regulations**. Steps taken include:

- **Data anonymization** before training and inference.
- **Role-based access control (RBAC)** for all data and model endpoints.
- **Private Link and VNet integration** for network isolation.
- **Audit logging** of all data access and model inference events.
- **Key Vault** to secure credentials and certificates.
- A **Business Associate Agreement (BAA)** signed with Microsoft.

Monitoring and Feedback Loop

Performance is monitored using Azure Application Insights:

- Latency and throughput of inference requests.
- Error rates and model exceptions.
- Resource utilization on AKS clusters.

Feedback from clinicians is used to:

- Flag false positives and false negatives.
- Retrain models periodically.
- Improve UX and trust through iteration.

Impact and Outcomes

- **Time to diagnosis** reduced by 35% in emergency cases.
- **Radiologist throughput** increased by 22% without additional staff.
- **Diagnostic accuracy** improved, especially in early pneumonia cases.
- **Clinician satisfaction** rated at 8.7/10 based on surveys.
- **Audit compliance** passed with zero critical findings.

Lessons Learned

1. **Interdisciplinary collaboration** is essential—data scientists, clinicians, and IT must co-design workflows.

2. **Model transparency** builds trust—clinicians are more likely to adopt AI if they understand it.

3. **Edge cases matter**—clinical data can be noisy, incomplete, or rare.

4. **Continuous monitoring** is key—models can drift as clinical patterns change.

5. **Security and privacy** cannot be retrofitted—they must be built in from the start.

Summary

This smart healthcare case study illustrates the powerful synergy between AI and Azure cloud technologies in a high-stakes environment. With a carefully planned architecture, responsible AI practices, robust compliance controls, and clinician engagement, AI becomes a force multiplier for human expertise.

By following the patterns demonstrated here, other healthcare organizations can implement similar solutions tailored to their specialties, from radiology and cardiology to oncology and mental health. The next section will explore another high-impact domain—retail and e-commerce—where AI is revolutionizing the customer journey and supply chain.

Case Study: AI in Retail and E-Commerce

The retail and e-commerce sectors have undergone rapid digital transformation, accelerated further by global shifts in consumer behavior and expectations. Artificial Intelligence (AI) now plays a critical role in driving personalized experiences, optimizing operations, managing supply chains, enhancing customer support, and boosting revenue. In this case study, we explore how a leading online retail enterprise leveraged the Microsoft Azure ecosystem to design, build, and scale a suite of AI-powered solutions that revolutionized their customer engagement strategy and operational efficiency.

This section will cover real-world implementations of AI technologies in a retail context, including product recommendation engines, customer segmentation, intelligent chatbots, dynamic pricing models, and demand forecasting—while ensuring data privacy, scalability, and maintainability.

Business Goals and Objectives

A multinational e-commerce retailer set out to achieve the following objectives:

- **Increase conversion rates and cart value** using hyper-personalized product recommendations.

- **Segment customers intelligently** for targeted marketing and promotions.

- **Provide 24/7 multilingual support** using AI-driven virtual assistants.

- **Optimize pricing strategies** dynamically based on competitor data and demand.

- **Improve demand forecasting** to reduce overstock and stockouts.

- **Ensure compliance** with global data privacy laws like GDPR and CCPA.

To achieve these goals, the company chose Microsoft Azure for its scalability, data capabilities, AI toolkits, and integrated security.

Architecture Overview

The AI infrastructure deployed across Azure follows a modular microservices architecture with clearly defined pipelines and real-time streaming capabilities.

Key Azure Components:

- **Azure Data Lake Storage Gen2**: Centralized storage for product, transaction, and clickstream data.

- **Azure Synapse Analytics**: Perform big data queries and joins across multiple sources.

- **Azure Machine Learning**: Train and deploy custom recommendation and segmentation models.

- **Azure Databricks**: ETL pipelines, Spark-based batch processing, and feature engineering.

- **Azure Cognitive Services**: Power intelligent search, sentiment analysis, and language translation.

- **Azure Functions**: Handle real-time triggers (e.g., cart abandonment alerts).

- **Azure Kubernetes Service (AKS)**: Host real-time model inference services with autoscaling.

- **Azure App Configuration and Key Vault**: Manage feature toggles and secrets securely.

- **Azure DevOps**: CI/CD for model versioning and deployment automation.

Use Case 1: Personalized Product Recommendations

Data Sources

- User   browsing   history

- Past   purchases

- Product   catalog   metadata   (category,   price,   availability,   ratings)

- Real-time   clickstream   and   cart   activity

Model Design

The solution implements a **hybrid recommender system** using:

- **Collaborative Filtering**: Matrix factorization based on user-item interactions.

- **Content-Based Filtering**: Using product descriptions, embeddings, and tags.

- **Real-Time Personalization**: Session-aware ranking using recent actions.

Azure ML pipelines train the model weekly on enriched feature datasets stored in Data Lake and precompute recommendation embeddings.

```python
from azureml.train.automl import AutoMLConfig

automl_config = AutoMLConfig(
    task='recommendation',
    primary_metric='normalized_discounted_cumulative_gain_at_k',
    training_data=training_df,
    label_column_name='rating',
    n_cross_validations=3,
    experiment_timeout_minutes=60
```

)

Deployment

The final ensemble model is deployed as a REST API on AKS, which integrates with the frontend web and mobile apps. Users receive tailored recommendations on the homepage, product pages, and checkout screens.

Use Case 2: Intelligent Customer Segmentation

The retailer uses clustering to identify and segment customers based on their behavior and demographics.

Data Points Used:

- Recency, Frequency, Monetary (RFM) scores
- Device and channel usage
- Browsing categories
- Conversion rates
- Return and refund patterns

Using Azure Databricks and MLflow, the data science team builds a K-Means clustering model that automatically updates weekly.

```
from sklearn.cluster import KMeans

kmeans = KMeans(n_clusters=5, random_state=42)
customer_segments = kmeans.fit_predict(features)
```

The segments are:

1. High-Value Frequent Buyers
2. Discount Shoppers
3. New Explorers
4. One-Time Purchasers

5. Inactive   Users

These segments are used to personalize email campaigns, promotions, and site experiences via API integration with the CMS.

Use Case 3: Multilingual AI Chatbots

To handle a global audience, the company implemented intelligent virtual assistants in 15 languages using **Azure Bot Service** and **Language Understanding (LUIS)**.

Features:

- Order   tracking

- Return   processing

- FAQ   resolution

- Real-time   escalation   to   human   agents

- Voice   input   support   on   mobile

Architecture Highlights:

- LUIS   models   trained   for   each   language   and   locale

- Azure   Cognitive   Services   Translator   used   to   bridge   gaps

- Integration   with   **Power   Virtual   Agents**   for   low-code   updates

- Bot hosted on Azure App Service with API Management for control and scaling

```
"utterance": "Where is my order?",
"intent": "TrackOrder",
"entities": {
  "OrderId": "12345678"
}
```

The bot handles over 85% of Tier 1 queries automatically and reduces average resolution time by 40%.

Use Case 4: Dynamic Pricing Engine

Prices are dynamically adjusted based on:

- Competitor pricing scraped via API

- Real-time demand and supply

- Stock levels and aging inventory

- Seasonal trends

A regression model powered by **Azure Machine Learning** predicts the optimal price point per SKU. The results are stored in a Redis cache and pushed to the product catalog service every 15 minutes.

```
from sklearn.ensemble import GradientBoostingRegressor

model = GradientBoostingRegressor()
model.fit(X_train, y_train)
predicted_prices = model.predict(X_test)
```

This has led to a 9% increase in gross margin without negatively impacting conversion rates.

Use Case 5: Demand Forecasting

The supply chain team uses deep learning models (LSTM-based) trained on historical sales, seasonality, promotions, and external factors (e.g., holidays, weather).

The pipeline:

- Ingests daily sales data into **Azure Data Lake**

- Enriches with external features via **Data Factory**

- Trains models on **Azure Databricks**

- Outputs forecasts to **Azure SQL** for dashboards and ordering systems

Accuracy improved by 23%, reducing overstocking and stockouts by over 30% across 12 markets.

Compliance and Governance

To meet GDPR, CCPA, and other regional regulations:

- Personal data is anonymized where possible.
- Consent management is integrated into user journeys.
- **Azure Purview** tracks data lineage and classifications.
- API endpoints have rate limiting and OAuth2 scopes.
- **Azure Key Vault** stores all API keys and secrets.
- Access to training data and production models is governed via **RBAC** and **Managed Identities**.

Monitoring and Feedback Loops

Real-time monitoring is done via **Azure Monitor** and **Application Insights**.

- API latency and success rate
- Model drift detection (via data distribution checks)
- Feedback ingestion from NPS surveys and customer reviews

The DevOps pipeline includes retraining triggers if performance drops below a certain threshold or if product catalogs change significantly.

Results and Business Impact

- **Conversion rate** increased by 12% year-over-year.
- **Average cart size** grew by 18% due to improved recommendations.
- **Customer support costs** reduced by 35%.
- **Stockouts** dropped by 30%, improving delivery SLAs.
- **NPS** improved from 7.4 to 8.6 across key regions.

Lessons Learned

1. **Model explainability** matters—especially when prices or recommendations impact revenue.

2. **Cross-functional collaboration** between data scientists, marketers, and engineers is vital.

3. **Scalability planning** upfront saves time during holiday and campaign surges.

4. **Feedback loops** are crucial to sustain relevance and trust in AI predictions.

5. **Security and compliance** must be automated and constantly verified in a retail environment with frequent releases.

Summary

This case study demonstrates how Azure's AI and cloud services can be orchestrated to transform retail operations across marketing, support, logistics, and personalization. By embedding intelligence at every step of the customer journey—and ensuring it is secure, scalable, and compliant—organizations can deliver superior experiences while optimizing operations.

In the next section, we'll explore the technical details of deploying AI models using Azure Kubernetes Service (AKS), including CI/CD integration, GPU scaling, and security hardening for production workloads.

Deploying AI Models with Azure Kubernetes Service

As AI models mature from research to production, robust deployment strategies become crucial. Enterprises need scalable, resilient, and secure infrastructure to serve AI workloads in real time. Azure Kubernetes Service (AKS) has emerged as a premier platform for deploying AI models, thanks to its flexibility, native integration with Azure services, and support for GPU acceleration, autoscaling, and DevOps pipelines.

In this section, we explore how to deploy machine learning models to AKS, covering both real-time and batch inference scenarios. We will walk through the process of containerizing AI models, creating and managing AKS clusters, configuring autoscaling, handling authentication and security, integrating CI/CD pipelines, and monitoring live deployments.

Why Use AKS for Model Deployment?

AKS is a fully managed Kubernetes service that simplifies the deployment and operations of containerized applications. For AI, it offers:

- **Scalability**: Automatic scaling of inference pods based on load.

- **Isolation**: Run models in separate namespaces or clusters.

- **GPU Support**: Accelerate inference with NVIDIA GPUs.

- **CI/CD Integration**: Automate deployment pipelines using GitHub or Azure DevOps.

- **Security**: RBAC, network policies, and private endpoints.

- **Observability**: Real-time logging, metrics, and tracing.

AKS is ideal when:

- You need to serve multiple models in production.

- You require fine-grained control over the environment.

- You need to support custom hardware, libraries, or dependencies.

Containerizing the Model

Start by creating a Docker container that packages your trained model, dependencies, and inference logic.

Example: Flask-based Python Inference API

```
from flask import Flask, request, jsonify
import joblib

app = Flask(__name__)
model = joblib.load("model.pkl")

@app.route("/predict", methods=["POST"])
def predict():
    data = request.json["data"]
    prediction = model.predict([data])
    return jsonify({"prediction": prediction.tolist()})
```

Dockerfile

```
FROM python:3.9-slim

WORKDIR /app
COPY requirements.txt ./
RUN pip install -r requirements.txt
COPY . .

CMD ["python", "app.py"]
```

Build and push the image to Azure Container Registry (ACR):

```
az acr build --registry myacr --image mlmodel:latest .
```

Creating an AKS Cluster

Create an AKS cluster with optional GPU nodes for intensive inference:

```
az aks create \
  --resource-group ai-rg \
  --name ai-aks-cluster \
  --node-count 3 \
  --enable-addons monitoring \
  --generate-ssh-keys \
  --node-vm-size Standard_DS3_v2
```

For GPU support:

```
az aks create \
  --resource-group ai-rg \
  --name gpu-aks-cluster \
  --node-count 2 \
  --node-vm-size Standard_NC6 \
  --enable-addons monitoring \
  --enable-managed-identity
```

Connect to the cluster:

```
az aks get-credentials --resource-group ai-rg --name ai-aks-cluster
```

Deploying the Model to AKS

Create a deployment and service definition in Kubernetes:

ml-deployment.yaml

```yaml
apiVersion: apps/v1
kind: Deployment
metadata:
  name: ml-model
spec:
  replicas: 2
  selector:
    matchLabels:
      app: ml-model
  template:
    metadata:
      labels:
        app: ml-model
    spec:
      containers:
      - name: ml-model
        image: myacr.azurecr.io/mlmodel:latest
        ports:
        - containerPort: 5000
---
apiVersion: v1
kind: Service
metadata:
  name: ml-model-service
spec:
  selector:
    app: ml-model
  ports:
  - protocol: TCP
    port: 80
    targetPort: 5000
  type: LoadBalancer
```

Apply the configuration:

```
kubectl apply -f ml-deployment.yaml
```

Retrieve the public IP:

```
kubectl get service ml-model-service
```

You can now send predictions to your endpoint via REST.

Autoscaling and Resource Management

Enable **Horizontal Pod Autoscaler (HPA)** based on CPU usage:

```
kubectl autoscale deployment ml-model --cpu-percent=60 --min=2 --max=10
```

For GPU-enabled workloads, ensure node pools have the correct **taints and tolerations**:

gpu-node-pool.yaml

```
tolerations:
- key: "sku"
  operator: "Equal"
  value: "gpu"
  effect: "NoSchedule"
```

Create node pools separately using:

```
az aks nodepool add \
  --resource-group ai-rg \
  --cluster-name ai-aks-cluster \
  --name gpu \
  --node-count 1 \
  --node-vm-size Standard_NC6 \
  --node-taints sku=gpu:NoSchedule
```

Authentication and Security

Secure your AKS model endpoints using:

- **Ingress + Application Gateway** with TLS
- **Azure Active Directory Pod Identity** for services needing secure data access
- **Network Policies** to control traffic between services

Use secrets from **Azure Key Vault** via Kubernetes secrets:

```
kubectl create secret generic kv-secret \
  --from-literal=API_KEY=$(az keyvault secret show --name mykey --
vault-name myvault --query value -o tsv)
```

Monitoring and Logging

Enable observability using:

- **Azure Monitor for Containers**
- **Prometheus + Grafana**
- **Application Insights**

Attach monitoring to the cluster during setup or post-configuration.

You can inspect logs for your container:

```
kubectl logs -f deployment/ml-model
```

Set up alerts for:

- Pod failures
- High latency
- Autoscaler limits
- CPU/GPU resource pressure

CI/CD with Azure DevOps or GitHub Actions

Create an automated deployment pipeline:

- **Trigger**: On model registry update or code push
- **Build Stage**: Build Docker image and push to ACR
- **Deploy Stage**: Apply updated manifests to AKS

GitHub Actions Workflow Example

```
jobs:
  deploy:
    runs-on: ubuntu-latest
    steps:
    - uses: azure/docker-login@v1
      with:
        login-server: myacr.azurecr.io
        username: ${{ secrets.ACR_USERNAME }}
        password: ${{ secrets.ACR_PASSWORD }}
    - run: |
        docker build -t myacr.azurecr.io/mlmodel:latest .
        docker push myacr.azurecr.io/mlmodel:latest
    - uses: azure/k8s-deploy@v1
      with:
        manifests: |
          ./k8s/ml-deployment.yaml
```

This ensures your model goes from training to production with traceability and rollback support.

Blue-Green and Canary Deployments

Avoid downtime and reduce risk by using advanced deployment strategies:

- **Blue-Green**: Maintain two environments; switch traffic after validation.
- **Canary**: Gradually shift traffic from old to new version.

Use tools like **Argo Rollouts**, **Flagger**, or native Kubernetes support with Ingress controllers to manage these patterns.

Cost Optimization

- Use **spot instances** for non-critical or retraining jobs.

- Scale node pools down during off-peak hours.

- Monitor container CPU/memory usage to optimize resource requests.

- Use **Azure Reservations** or **Savings Plans** for predictable workloads.

Summary

Azure Kubernetes Service provides a robust, flexible platform for deploying AI models at scale. By containerizing models and leveraging Kubernetes orchestration, organizations gain full control over the performance, security, and scalability of their AI services.

From GPU acceleration and autoscaling to secure network policies and CI/CD pipelines, AKS supports the full lifecycle of model deployment in production environments. Whether your AI workload involves image recognition, recommendation systems, or natural language processing, AKS ensures that your solution is production-grade, maintainable, and future-proof.

In the next section, we'll explore how Azure Arc can extend these AI capabilities to hybrid and multi-cloud environments—enabling intelligent applications wherever your data lives.

Using Azure Arc for Hybrid AI Deployment

In today's increasingly distributed IT landscape, many organizations operate across hybrid environments—combining on-premises infrastructure, multiple public clouds, and edge devices. These setups present unique challenges for deploying AI workloads consistently and securely across environments. Azure Arc, a core component of Microsoft's hybrid cloud strategy, addresses these challenges by enabling unified management, governance, and deployment of applications and services across heterogeneous infrastructure.

Azure Arc brings Azure services to any infrastructure, allowing organizations to deploy and manage AI solutions on premises, in other clouds, or at the edge using the same toolset, policies, and security models used in Azure. This section explores how Azure Arc enables hybrid AI deployment, including model deployment to Kubernetes clusters outside Azure, integration with Azure Machine Learning, centralized governance, and real-world hybrid scenarios.

The Case for Hybrid AI

Several factors drive the need for hybrid AI deployments:

- **Data Sovereignty**: Regulations require that certain data remain within a specific geographic region or facility.

- **Latency Requirements**: Real-time applications, such as predictive maintenance on manufacturing equipment, demand inference at the edge.

- **Legacy Infrastructure**: Some organizations operate within highly specialized on-premises environments that cannot be migrated easily.

- **Multi-Cloud Strategy**: Enterprises aiming to avoid vendor lock-in or leverage specific services from different providers.

- **Operational Consistency**: Teams want to use the same tooling across environments to avoid skill fragmentation.

Azure Arc bridges these gaps by extending Azure's capabilities beyond its native data centers.

What Is Azure Arc?

Azure Arc is a set of technologies that extends Azure services and management to infrastructure outside of Azure. Key features include:

- **Arc-enabled Kubernetes**: Connect and manage any CNCF-compliant Kubernetes cluster with Azure.

- **Arc-enabled Servers**: Bring Azure management capabilities to Windows and Linux servers anywhere.

- **Arc-enabled Data Services**: Deploy Azure SQL and PostgreSQL Hyperscale outside Azure.

- **Arc-enabled Machine Learning**: Run ML models and training jobs on hybrid or multi-cloud infrastructure.

Azure Arc enables developers to treat on-prem and multi-cloud environments as first-class Azure citizens.

Arc-Enabled Kubernetes for AI Inference

A central use case of Azure Arc in AI is deploying trained models to Kubernetes clusters running on-premises or in another cloud.

Step 1: Connect Your Kubernetes Cluster

Ensure your cluster is CNCF-compliant and has outbound internet access.

```
az connectedk8s connect \
  --name arc-ai-cluster \
  --resource-group hybrid-rg \
  --location eastus
```

The cluster now appears in the Azure Portal and supports:

- Azure   Policy   enforcement

- GitOps-based   configuration

- Role-Based   Access   Control   (RBAC)

- Monitoring   with   Azure   Monitor   for   Containers

Step 2: Enable Azure ML Extension

```
az k8s-extension create \
  --name aml-extension \
  --cluster-name arc-ai-cluster \
  --resource-group hybrid-rg \
  --cluster-type connectedClusters \
  --extension-type Microsoft.AzureML.Kubernetes
```

This registers the cluster as a compute target in Azure Machine Learning.

Step 3: Deploy Models from Azure ML

Once connected, you can deploy models trained in Azure ML Studio directly to the Arc-enabled cluster.

```
from azureml.core.compute import KubernetesCompute

compute_config = AksCompute.attach_configuration(
    resource_group="hybrid-rg",
    cluster_name="arc-ai-cluster"
)
compute_target = ComputeTarget.attach(workspace=ws, name="arc-cluster", attach_configuration=compute_config)
compute_target.wait_for_completion(show_output=True)
```

Now register a model and deploy it to the Arc cluster:

```python
from azureml.core.model import InferenceConfig, Model

model = Model(workspace=ws, name="hybrid-recommender")
inference_config       =       InferenceConfig(entry_script="score.py",
environment=environment)

deployment_config  =  AksWebservice.deploy_configuration(cpu_cores=2,
memory_gb=4)

service = Model.deploy(workspace=ws,
                       name="recommendation-service",
                       models=[model],
                       inference_config=inference_config,
                       deployment_config=deployment_config,
                       deployment_target=compute_target)
```

GitOps for Consistent Model Deployment

Azure Arc supports **GitOps** via **Flux v2**, allowing you to define model deployments as code and synchronize them across environments.

Example: model-deployment.yaml

```yaml
apiVersion: apps/v1
kind: Deployment
metadata:
  name: hybrid-model
spec:
  replicas: 2
  selector:
    matchLabels:
      app: hybrid-model
  template:
    metadata:
      labels:
        app: hybrid-model
    spec:
      containers:
```

```yaml
- name: hybrid-model
  image: myacr.azurecr.io/recommender:v1
  ports:
  - containerPort: 5000
```

You can commit the above YAML to GitHub and configure Arc to watch and apply changes automatically.

```
az k8s-configuration create \
  --name hybrid-gitops \
  --cluster-name arc-ai-cluster \
  --resource-group hybrid-rg \
  --cluster-type connectedClusters \
  --operator-instance-name flux \
  --operator-namespace flux-system \
  --repository-url https://github.com/myorg/ai-deployments \
  --scope cluster \
  --enable-helm-operator
```

This enables reproducible, policy-compliant deployments for machine learning services at scale.

Data Considerations for Hybrid AI

Data locality is critical in hybrid AI. You may not be able to move sensitive datasets to Azure, so inference and even training may need to run where the data lives.

Options include:

- **Training on-prem** using Arc-enabled ML compute

- **Using Azure ML pipelines to trigger jobs remotely**

- **Data sync with Azure Data Box or Azure File Sync**

You can store logs, metrics, or anonymized features in Azure while maintaining raw data residency locally.

Observability and Governance

Azure Arc supports centralized logging and governance:

- **Azure Monitor for Containers**: Extend logging and metrics to non-Azure clusters.

- **Azure Policy for Kubernetes**: Apply policies like allowed container registries, namespace quotas, or pod security standards.

- **Azure Defender**: Extend threat detection and security baselines to Arc-connected environments.

Use **Azure Lighthouse** for multi-tenant governance in managed service provider (MSP) scenarios.

Real-World Use Case: Retail Edge AI

A global retailer uses Azure Arc to deploy AI models for real-time shelf inventory tracking in 3,000 stores.

Setup:

- Models trained in Azure and exported as ONNX files.

- In-store edge servers running Arc-enabled Kubernetes clusters.

- Cameras feed images to object detection models (e.g., YOLOv5).

- Prediction results update local dashboards and sync with Azure SQL.

Benefits:

- Compliance with local data residency laws

- Zero dependency on continuous internet

- GitOps deployment of model updates

- Central monitoring of all stores

Benefits of Azure Arc for AI

Benefit	Description

Unified Management	Manage all clusters from the Azure Portal regardless of location
Consistency	Use the same deployment tools, policies, and pipelines across environments
Scalability	Add capacity wherever needed, including edge and other cloud providers
Compliance	Enforce governance even outside Azure using Azure Policy
Portability	Avoid vendor lock-in by using CNCF-compliant Kubernetes
Flexibility	Run AI anywhere your data or customers are located

Summary

Azure Arc revolutionizes how organizations approach hybrid and multi-cloud AI deployment. By bridging the gap between on-premises systems, public cloud, and edge environments, Arc allows you to bring your models and data science practices wherever they are needed—without sacrificing manageability, security, or compliance.

With Arc, deploying models to retail stores, factory floors, financial branches, or hospital data centers becomes as seamless as deploying within Azure. This approach ensures that AI is truly ubiquitous, adaptive, and resilient—unlocking the full potential of intelligent applications across the modern enterprise.

In the next chapter, we'll turn our attention to optimizing the performance and cost-efficiency of AI workloads in Azure—ensuring that your models are not only powerful but also sustainable and budget-conscious.

Chapter 9: Performance Optimization and Cost Management

Optimizing AI Workloads in Azure

Optimizing AI workloads in Azure is a multi-dimensional challenge that encompasses computational efficiency, model performance, latency, infrastructure usage, and operational overhead. As AI models grow in complexity and deployment environments diversify, it becomes essential to adopt a structured approach to optimize these workloads for both performance and cost-effectiveness.

This section explores the strategies, tools, and architectural patterns that can significantly improve the efficiency of training, inference, data handling, and system operations. We'll address practical ways to optimize GPU and CPU usage, reduce storage I/O, accelerate pipelines, use the right VM types, leverage auto-scaling, and choose the most effective data architecture for your AI solutions.

Dimensions of Optimization

Optimization spans across the following key dimensions:

- **Compute Optimization**: Choosing the right VM sizes, using autoscaling, leveraging GPU acceleration effectively.

- **Model Optimization**: Pruning, quantization, distillation, and batching techniques.

- **Storage Optimization**: Improving I/O throughput, caching, and choosing suitable data formats.

- **Pipeline Optimization**: Minimizing redundant operations in data processing and inference.

- **Deployment Optimization**: Using serverless functions for infrequent inference or AKS for high-scale, low-latency use cases.

- **Network Optimization**: Reducing data transfer overhead between services.

A holistic performance strategy ensures that gains in one area don't create bottlenecks elsewhere.

Optimizing Model Training

1. Choose the Right Compute Type

For training deep learning models:

- Use **Azure Machine Learning GPU-enabled VMs** such as `Standard_NC6` or `Standard_ND40rs_v2`.

- Use **Azure ML Compute Clusters** to enable auto-scaling based on queue size.

- Use **Low Priority (Spot) VMs** for cost-effective training jobs with checkpointing.

```
from azureml.core.compute import AmlCompute, ComputeTarget

compute_config = AmlCompute.provisioning_configuration(
    vm_size='STANDARD_NC6',
    min_nodes=0,
    max_nodes=4,
    idle_seconds_before_scaledown=300
)
```

2. Use Data Parallelism and Distributed Training

Distribute training using Horovod, PyTorch DDP, or TensorFlow MultiWorkerMirroredStrategy.

```
import horovod.tensorflow.keras as hvd
hvd.init()
```

Azure ML supports these configurations natively through `distributed_training` in the `ScriptRunConfig`.

3. Optimize Data I/O

- Cache frequently accessed datasets with **Azure Blob Storage's Premium tier**.

- Use **Parquet** or **TFRecord** formats instead of CSV for high-speed access.

- Use **Data Versioning** to avoid duplicating large datasets during iteration.

Optimizing Inference Workloads

1. Use ONNX for Efficient Inference

ONNX (Open Neural Network Exchange) allows you to export models to a highly optimized format that runs faster on CPU and GPU.

```
import torch.onnx
torch.onnx.export(model, input_sample, "model.onnx")
```

Deploy using ONNX Runtime in Azure Functions, Azure ML Endpoints, or AKS.

2. Implement Batching

Batch multiple inference requests together to increase throughput:

```
def batch_predict(inputs):
    batched_inputs = torch.stack(inputs)
    return model(batched_inputs)
```

Use Azure ML's batch endpoints for asynchronous batch scoring.

3. Use Model Quantization and Pruning

Quantize models to lower precision (e.g., float32 → int8) to reduce size and improve performance.

Use tools like **ONNX Runtime Quantization Tool** or **TensorRT** for this purpose.

Pipeline and Workflow Optimization

1. Reuse Precomputed Features

- Store and reuse engineered features to avoid redundant computation.
- Use **Azure Feature Store (preview)** or Azure Data Lake for this purpose.

2. Cache Intermediate Results

Use caching within Azure Machine Learning pipelines to skip unnecessary re-computation:

```
@pipeline_step(cache=True)
def preprocess_data():
    ...
```

3. Use Parallelism in Data Prep

Azure ML supports **parallel pipeline steps** and **parallel batch scoring** to maximize throughput.

Infrastructure Optimization Strategies

1. Use Azure Functions for Serverless Inference

For low-frequency or event-driven inference, deploy models as serverless endpoints:

- Cost-effective

- Scales to zero when idle

- Simple to deploy via containerized HTTP APIs

2. Use Azure Kubernetes Service (AKS) for Heavy Inference

AKS provides high scalability, GPU support, and better control over infrastructure. Use it when:

- Models require real-time latency

- You need to scale rapidly

- You're handling large batch jobs

3. Right-Size VM and Storage Tiers

- Use **Standard SSD** for moderate IOPS

- Use **Premium SSD** or **Ultra Disk** for high throughput workloads

- Use **Premium Files** or **Blob Storage** for large datasets

- Avoid over-provisioning; benchmark before scaling up

Monitoring and Telemetry

Use **Azure Monitor**, **Log Analytics**, and **Application Insights** to:

- Track inference latency

- Observe compute utilization

- Alert on abnormal errors or performance drops

```
requests
| where name contains "predict"
| summarize avg(duration) by bin(timestamp, 5m)
```

Enable **Prometheus + Grafana** for detailed Kubernetes (AKS) metrics.

Model Performance Tuning

1. Hyperparameter Tuning

Use Azure ML's HyperDrive for scalable tuning:

```
from azureml.train.hyperdrive import RandomParameterSampling, HyperDriveConfig

param_sampling = RandomParameterSampling({
    'learning_rate': uniform(0.001, 0.1),
    'batch_size': choice(16, 32, 64)
})
```

2. Reduce Model Complexity

- Consider smaller architectures like MobileNet, SqueezeNet for mobile/edge.

- Use model pruning and knowledge distillation to retain accuracy while improving speed.

3. Evaluate Trade-offs

- High accuracy vs. inference latency

- Throughput vs. cost

- Explainability vs. performance

Leveraging Azure-Specific Tools

Tool	Purpose
Azure Machine Learning	Model training, deployment, tracking
Azure Monitor	Log and performance analytics
Azure Advisor	Recommends performance and cost improvements
Azure Cost Management	Budgeting, forecasting, and cost analysis
Azure Policy	Enforce resource usage rules and optimization
Azure Spot VMs	Lower-cost compute for non-critical tasks
Azure Batch AI	Scalable batch inference and processing

Best Practices Checklist

Area	Best Practice
Compute	Use spot instances and scale-to-zero where possible
Inference	Use ONNX, quantization, and batch prediction
Data	Use efficient formats like Parquet and avoid redundant copies
Storage	Choose appropriate performance tier for I/O needs
Monitoring	Set up latency, error, and usage alerts
Optimization Tools	Use Azure ML HyperDrive and Model Interpretability
Cost Control	Track budgets using Azure Cost Management and enforce quotas via policies

Summary

Performance optimization is not a one-time effort—it's an ongoing discipline. With Azure's rich toolset and services, you can proactively monitor, refine, and scale AI workloads while ensuring operational efficiency and cost control.

By choosing the right compute resources, optimizing models and data pipelines, automating scaling, and applying the right telemetry, organizations can deliver high-performing, low-cost AI systems tailored to their needs.

In the next section, we will shift our focus toward financial optimization—learning how to conduct cost analysis, set budgets, and plan sustainable AI operations in Azure.

Cost Analysis and Budgeting Strategies

Running AI workloads in the cloud can yield immense value, but without proper cost governance, organizations may face budget overruns, unexpected billing spikes, and inefficiencies that erode ROI. AI systems often rely on resource-intensive services—such as GPUs, large-scale data pipelines, and high-throughput inference endpoints—that must be actively monitored, optimized, and aligned with strategic financial plans.

This section presents a structured approach to performing cost analysis and implementing budgeting strategies for AI workloads in Azure. We will examine how to track and predict AI-related spending, allocate budgets across teams or projects, analyze cost drivers, and enforce usage policies. Leveraging Azure-native tools like Cost Management + Billing, Azure Reservations, Azure Hybrid Benefit, and tagging strategies, organizations can optimize spending while ensuring operational continuity.

Understanding the Components of AI Cost in Azure

AI workloads span multiple services, each contributing to the overall cost:

- **Compute Costs**: VM instances (CPU/GPU), Azure ML compute clusters, AKS nodes, Azure Functions, Logic Apps.

- **Storage Costs**: Azure Blob Storage, Data Lake Gen2, Premium SSDs, File Shares.

- **Data Transfer Costs**: Egress from Azure regions, VNet peering, CDN, API Gateway calls.

- **Service Costs**: Azure Machine Learning usage, Cognitive Services API calls, Databricks, Synapse usage.

- **Monitoring Costs**: Azure Monitor, Application Insights, Log Analytics storage.

Each service may use different pricing models: per second, per call, per GB, or per SU (streaming units), making it critical to normalize and aggregate these metrics across workloads.

Azure Cost Management and Billing

Azure provides a built-in suite of tools for tracking, analyzing, and forecasting costs.

1. Viewing and Analyzing Costs

Navigate to **Cost Management + Billing** in the Azure Portal:

- Set **Scope**: subscription, resource group, or management group.

- Filter by **resource type**, **location**, or **tags**.

- View **accumulated cost**, **forecast**, and **cost by resource/service**.

Example: View AI service costs over the last 30 days

```
UsageDetails
| where ResourceType contains "MachineLearning" or ResourceType
contains "CognitiveServices"
| summarize TotalCost = sum(PreTaxCost) by ResourceGroup,
MeterCategory, bin(UsageDate, 1d)
```

2. Forecasting and Alerts

Use the **Forecast** tab to estimate future spending based on current trends. Set up **budget alerts** to stay within defined thresholds.

```
az consumption budget create \
  --amount 5000 \
  --category cost \
  --name ai-budget \
  --resource-group ai-rg \
  --time-grain monthly \
  --start-date 2024-01-01 \
  --end-date 2025-01-01 \
  --notifications                enabled=true                threshold=90
contactEmails=finance@company.com
```

Budgeting Strategies for AI Projects

1. Allocate Budgets by Team, Project, or Department

Use **resource groups**, **subscriptions**, or **Azure Management Groups** to segregate billing scopes.

Example structure:

- `AI-Research-RG`   – R&D   experimentation
- `AI-Production-RG`   – Production   endpoints   and   models
- `DataEngineering-RG`   – ETL   pipelines   and   storage

Assign budgets and quotas to each using Cost Management.

2. Implement Tagging Policies

Tag all AI-related resources for traceability.

```
az tag create \
  --resource-id /subscriptions/<sub-id>/resourceGroups/AI-Project \
  --tags Project=RecommendationEngine Owner=Frahaan CostCenter=AI123
```

Tag examples:

- `Project, Environment, CostCenter, Owner, ModelType, UseCase`

Use **Azure Policy** to enforce mandatory tags on creation.

Identifying and Reducing Cost Drivers

1. Idle or Underutilized Compute

- Use   Azure   Advisor   to   identify   VMs   with   low   usage.
- Review   AKS   node   pools   and   cluster   usage   during   non-peak   hours.
- Configure   **scale-to-zero**   or   **auto-shutdown**   for   ML   compute   clusters.

2. Storage Redundancy

- Archive old logs to **Cool** or **Archive** storage tiers.
- Use **Lifecycle** **Management** **Rules** to delete unused blobs:

```json
{
  "rules": [
    {
      "enabled": true,
      "name": "archive-old-data",
      "type": "Lifecycle",
      "definition": {
        "actions": {
          "baseBlob": {
            "tierToCool": { "daysAfterModificationGreaterThan": 30 },
            "tierToArchive": { "daysAfterModificationGreaterThan": 90 },
            "delete": { "daysAfterModificationGreaterThan": 365 }
          }
        },
        "filters": { "blobTypes": [ "blockBlob" ] }
      }
    }
  ]
}
```

3. Inefficient Inference Workloads

- Right-size endpoints: use **smaller** **VMs** or batch endpoints.
- Auto-scale AKS inference pods based on CPU/GPU usage.
- Consolidate models using **multi-model** **hosting** if supported.

4. Cognitive Services Cost Optimization

- Bundle services under **Azure Cognitive Services multi-service resource**.
- Monitor quotas and rotate keys securely.
- Cache results of frequent queries to reduce API calls.

Using Reservations and Hybrid Benefits

1. Azure Reserved Instances (RI)

Commit to one-year or three-year plans for predictable workloads:

```
az reservations reservation-order purchase \
  --sku "Standard_NC6s_v3" \
  --term "P1Y" \
  --billing-scope-id /subscriptions/<sub-id>
```

Savings: up to 72% compared to pay-as-you-go.

2. Azure Hybrid Benefit

Use existing on-prem Windows Server or SQL Server licenses with Azure:

- Apply to VM-based inference services or Azure SQL used in AI pipelines.

- Activated in VM creation wizard or via CLI.

Implementing a FinOps Culture

FinOps (Financial Operations) encourages cross-functional ownership of cloud spend.

Key tenets:

- **Visibility**: Dashboards for engineers and finance teams.

- **Optimization**: Continuous review and tuning of resources.

- **Accountability**: Chargeback or showback mechanisms.

- **Automation**: Auto-scaling, shutdown policies, alerts.

Use tools like:

- **Azure DevOps Dashboards**

- **Power BI with Cost Management APIs**

- **Third-party FinOps platforms** (e.g., CloudHealth, CloudCheckr)

Real-World Example: AI Budget Optimization

A fintech company running credit scoring models in Azure ML reduced costs by 38% through:

- Switching from premium compute to spot VMs for retraining jobs.
- Using ONNX and Azure Functions for lightweight inference.
- Moving 12 TB of log data from Hot to Archive tier.
- Implementing a GitOps policy to delete non-tagged resources nightly.
- Setting department-level budgets with 80% alert thresholds.

This enabled faster innovation without sacrificing financial discipline.

Best Practices for Budgeting and Cost Control

Practice	Description
Use Cost Management	Visualize usage and trends per resource or tag
Set Budgets and Alerts	Proactively manage overages
Apply Reservations	Save on predictable workloads
Leverage Spot VMs	Reduce cost for interruptible or batch training jobs
Enforce Shutdown Policies	Avoid overnight or weekend idle usage
Optimize Inference	Use batching, ONNX, or serverless where appropriate
Monitor Continuously	Integrate alerts into DevOps and incident response workflows
Implement Governance	Enforce tagging, RBAC, and policies for resource lifecycle management

Summary

Strategic cost analysis and budgeting are fundamental to sustainable AI operations in the cloud. By gaining visibility into spending, assigning ownership, forecasting usage, and implementing cost-saving techniques, organizations can extract maximum value from Azure AI services without financial surprises.

Azure's tools empower both technical and business stakeholders to collaborate, iterate, and scale AI workloads confidently while staying within budget. In the next section, we'll explore the tools available to monitor AI workloads in real time and implement auto-scaling strategies that ensure performance and cost-efficiency dynamically.

Tools for Monitoring and Auto-Scaling AI Services

Maintaining AI service performance, reliability, and cost-efficiency at scale requires robust monitoring and dynamic resource management. Azure offers a rich set of integrated tools that enable engineers to monitor machine learning pipelines, model endpoints, data pipelines, and infrastructure in real time. Combined with intelligent auto-scaling mechanisms, these tools help ensure your AI workloads remain responsive under varying loads while avoiding over-provisioning and wasted compute.

This section covers essential Azure tools and strategies for implementing monitoring and auto-scaling in AI solutions. We'll dive into telemetry collection, alerting systems, performance dashboards, resource scaling policies, and advanced techniques like anomaly detection and predictive scaling. Whether you're running models on Azure Kubernetes Service (AKS), Azure Machine Learning endpoints, Azure Functions, or custom VMs, this section provides the foundation to build scalable and observable AI systems.

Monitoring Goals for AI Workloads

Effective monitoring for AI workloads spans multiple domains:

- **Model Monitoring**: Track accuracy, drift, latency, and input anomalies.

- **Service Monitoring**: Measure CPU/GPU utilization, memory, and response times.

- **Data Pipeline Monitoring**: Ensure ingestion, transformation, and export processes run smoothly.

- **Security Monitoring**: Detect unauthorized access or misconfigurations.

- **Cost Monitoring**: Alert on cost thresholds or resource bloat.

Together, these metrics help you assess **system health**, **user experience**, and **model trustworthiness**.

Azure Monitor: The Central Hub

Azure Monitor is the core platform for collecting, analyzing, and acting on telemetry from Azure resources.

Key components:

- **Metrics**: Real-time numerical data (e.g., CPU %, inference time)

- **Logs**: Detailed events and traces using Kusto Query Language (KQL)

- **Alerts**: Rules that trigger actions when thresholds are breached

- **Workbooks**: Dashboards for visualization

- **Application Insights**: Deep application-level performance monitoring

Monitoring Azure Machine Learning Endpoints

Azure ML allows both **real-time** and **batch** endpoints. You can monitor:

- Number of requests

- Latency (P50, P95)

- Success/failure rates

- Input/output schema drift

- Endpoint uptime

Enabling Application Insights:

```
from azureml.core.webservice import AciWebservice

deployment_config = AciWebservice.deploy_configuration(
    cpu_cores=1,
    memory_gb=1,
    enable_app_insights=True
)
```

In Azure ML Studio, navigate to your endpoint → "Monitoring" to view live telemetry.

Sample KQL Query:

```
requests
| where name contains "predict"
| summarize avg(duration), count() by bin(timestamp, 5m)
```

Monitoring AKS-Based Inference Services

If deploying models via Azure Kubernetes Service (AKS), enable **Azure Monitor for Containers**.

Enable monitoring at cluster creation:

```
az aks create \
  --name aks-ai \
  --resource-group ai-rg \
  --enable-addons monitoring \
  --workspace-resource-id <log-analytics-id>
```

Metrics collected:

• Node	and	pod	CPU/memory	usage
• Disk	and		network	throughput
• Container		restart		count
• Namespace				quotas
• API	server		response	codes

You can also install **Prometheus and Grafana** on AKS for customized dashboards.

Alerting with Azure Monitor

Set up alerts to detect:

- High   inference   latency

- GPU saturation

- Model input anomalies

- Service unavailability

Example: Alert on average endpoint latency > 1000 ms

```
az monitor metrics alert create \
  --name latency-alert \
  --resource ai-endpoint \
  --condition "avg InferenceTime > 1000" \
  --window-size 5m \
  --evaluation-frequency 1m \
  --action-group NotifyTeam
```

Action Groups can notify via:

- Email, SMS, push notifications

- Azure Functions or Logic Apps

- ITSM or webhook integrations

Auto-Scaling with Azure Machine Learning

Azure ML compute clusters can **scale automatically** based on queued jobs:

```
from azureml.core.compute import AmlCompute

compute_config = AmlCompute.provisioning_configuration(
    vm_size="STANDARD_DS3_V2",
    min_nodes=0,
    max_nodes=8,
    idle_seconds_before_scaledown=600
)
```

Once idle for 10 minutes, nodes are automatically released—reducing cost.

Key parameters:

- `min_nodes:` Minimum baseline
- `max_nodes:` Burst capacity
- `idle_seconds_before_scaledown:` How soon to scale down after idle

Auto-Scaling in AKS

Use **Horizontal Pod Autoscaler (HPA)** for real-time inference workloads:

```
kubectl autoscale deployment inference-api \
  --cpu-percent=70 \
  --min=2 \
  --max=10
```

Auto-scaling triggers:

- CPU or memory usage
- Custom metrics via Prometheus Adapter
- Queue depth (using KEDA)

Vertical Pod Autoscaler (VPA) can also recommend resource limits per container.

Event-Driven Scaling with Azure Functions

For AI workloads triggered by events (e.g., file upload, webhook, API call), Azure Functions provide auto-scaling and pay-per-use execution.

Use **Durable Functions** for long-running ML workflows:

```
import azure.durable_functions as df

def orchestrator_function(context: df.DurableOrchestrationContext):
    result1 = yield context.call_activity("PreprocessData", None)
    result2 = yield context.call_activity("RunModel", result1)
    return result2
```

Functions scale to zero when not in use, ideal for low-traffic AI endpoints.

Monitoring Data Pipelines

Track pipeline executions via:

- **Azure** **Data** **Factory** **Monitoring** **View**

- **Azure** **Synapse** **Pipeline** **Monitoring**

- **Custom** **logs** **via** **Azure** **Log** **Analytics**

Enable diagnostic logs for Data Factory:

```
az monitor diagnostic-settings create \
  --resource                              /subscriptions/<sub-
id>/resourceGroups/<rg>/providers/Microsoft.DataFactory/factories/<f
actory> \
  --workspace <log-analytics-id> \
  --logs '[{"category":"PipelineRuns","enabled":true}]'
```

Model and Data Drift Monitoring

Use **Azure ML Data Drift Monitor** to detect changes in input data over time:

```
from azureml.datadrift import DataDriftDetector

detector = DataDriftDetector.create_from_datasets(
    workspace=ws,
    name='drift-detector',
    baseline_data_set=baseline_ds,
    target_data_set=current_ds,
    compute_target='cpu-cluster',
    features=['age', 'income', 'region']
)
```

Set up email alerts when drift is detected or accuracy drops beyond threshold.

Predictive Scaling with Metrics

Advanced teams implement predictive scaling by:

- Monitoring trends in traffic or usage patterns.

- Training time-series models (e.g., ARIMA, Prophet) on usage metrics.

- Using **Azure Automation Runbooks** to proactively scale compute ahead of time.

For example:

```
az ml compute update --name my-cluster --max-nodes 16
```

Triggered by a scheduled runbook based on weekly traffic forecast.

Visualization Tools

- **Azure Workbooks**: Create custom dashboards from Log Analytics data.

- **Power BI**: Connect to Azure Monitor and Cost Management for finance + ops views.

- **Grafana (Azure Managed)**: Visualize metrics from multiple Azure and custom sources.

Best Practices for Monitoring and Scaling

Practice	Benefit
Enable Metrics and Logs	Gain visibility into system behavior
Set Smart Alerts	Respond to issues before users are impacted
Use HPA and VPA in AKS	Adjust capacity based on real usage
Batch Inference When Possible	Improve throughput and lower per-request cost
Monitor Model Health	Detect accuracy degradation or drift over time

Implement Predictive Scaling	Prepare for known demand spikes in advance
Automate Shutdown Policies	Eliminate waste from idle resources
Tag and Segment Workloads	Attribute usage and performance by environment, model, or service

Summary

Proactive monitoring and intelligent auto-scaling are essential to running efficient, reliable, and cost-effective AI systems on Azure. Whether you're deploying models to Kubernetes, Azure Machine Learning, or serverless functions, Azure offers a robust ecosystem of tools to help you stay in control.

By leveraging metrics, alerts, scaling policies, and predictive models, you can ensure that your AI workloads scale to meet demand while remaining operationally efficient. In the next chapter, we'll explore the future of AI in Azure—including cutting-edge trends like quantum computing, edge AI, and how to continuously learn and evolve your AI strategies.

Chapter 10: The Future of AI in Azure

Trends and Innovations in AI on Azure

Artificial Intelligence (AI) is evolving rapidly, with advancements reshaping industries, redefining productivity, and driving new levels of human-computer interaction. As the frontier of innovation expands, Microsoft Azure continues to push the boundaries of AI by integrating cutting-edge capabilities into its cloud platform. These developments not only enable organizations to build smarter applications but also make AI more accessible, scalable, and trustworthy.

This section explores the future-facing trends and innovations in AI on Azure. It highlights the integration of large-scale foundation models, generative AI, responsible AI enhancements, low-code/no-code tools, multimodal systems, AutoML, AI agents, and more. We'll also examine how these technologies are becoming democratized through prebuilt APIs, customizable pipelines, and scalable infrastructure—positioning Azure as a strategic platform for next-generation AI workloads.

1. Foundation Models and Azure OpenAI Service

One of the most transformative developments in AI has been the rise of foundation models—large-scale, pretrained models capable of performing a wide array of tasks with minimal task-specific training. Microsoft Azure, in partnership with OpenAI, has operationalized this shift by offering the **Azure OpenAI Service**.

Key Capabilities

- **Language Understanding and Generation**: GPT-4, GPT-3.5

- **Code Assistance**: Codex, integrated into tools like GitHub Copilot

- **Chatbots and Virtual Agents**: Integrated with Azure Bot Service and Power Virtual Agents

- **Search + Generation (RAG)**: Combining Azure Cognitive Search with GPT models

Example Use Case:

```
import openai

openai.api_type = "azure"
openai.api_base = "https://<your-resource>.openai.azure.com/"
openai.api_key = "<your-key>"
```

```
openai.api_version = "2023-03-15-preview"

response = openai.ChatCompletion.create(
    engine="gpt-4",
    messages=[{"role": "user", "content": "Explain the difference
between reinforcement learning and supervised learning."}]
)
print(response.choices[0].message["content"])
```

Azure OpenAI empowers developers to build enterprise-ready generative applications while adhering to Microsoft's responsible AI standards and enterprise-grade security.

2. Generative AI and Prompt Engineering

Generative AI is transforming content creation, software development, data analysis, and customer engagement. Azure supports the development and deployment of generative AI systems through:

- **Prompt Engineering Tools**: Azure ML prompt flow and templates

- **Fine-tuning**: Customizing GPT models for domain-specific responses

- **Vector Search + AI**: Hybrid search using Azure Cognitive Search + embeddings

- **Safety Filters**: Built-in moderation and filtering layers

Prompt Flow in Azure ML

Prompt flow enables end-to-end management of prompt engineering, grounding, and evaluation:

- Design and chain prompts with tools like LangChain

- Evaluate with human-in-the-loop reviews

- Version, test, and deploy flows like standard ML models

This is critical for building chatbots, summarizers, assistants, and autonomous agents with structured workflows.

3. Multimodal AI Capabilities

The next generation of AI models will process and reason across multiple modalities:

- **Text**: GPT-4, BERT

- **Images**: DALL·E, CLIP, Azure Custom Vision

- **Audio**: Azure Speech-to-Text and Text-to-Speech

- **Video**: Azure Video Indexer

Azure supports multimodal pipelines for:

- Captioning and translating videos

- Creating image descriptions from alt text

- Building voice-enabled assistants with emotion detection

- Performing content moderation across video and text

Example: Use Azure Video Indexer to transcribe, translate, and extract key topics from recorded meetings.

---

4. AI Orchestration and Autonomous Agents

AI is moving beyond static models toward **autonomous agents**—systems that can reason, plan, and act on behalf of users. Azure enables these capabilities through:

- **Semantic Kernel**: A framework for integrating AI models with memory, tools, and goals

- **Orchestration Engines**: LangChain, Semantic Kernel, Copilot stack

- **Azure Bot Framework Composer**: For intent-driven conversational design

Example scenario: A supply chain AI agent that can proactively reorder stock, forecast demand, and alert logistics teams based on dynamic thresholds—powered by Azure ML and cognitive services.

---

5. Low-Code/No-Code AI with Azure

To make AI development accessible to more users, Azure continues to expand its low-code/no-code offerings:

- **Azure ML Designer**: Drag-and-drop interface for building and training models

- **Power Platform AI Builder**: For citizen developers to integrate AI into apps

- **Custom Vision** and **Form Recognizer Studio**: GUI-based model training

These tools empower business analysts, operations teams, and students to build intelligent apps without needing deep ML expertise.

---

6. AutoML and Custom Model Training

AutoML on Azure continues to evolve with:

- **Time   Series   Forecasting**   enhancements

- **Explainable   AutoML**   for   transparency

- **AutoML   for   Images**   for   computer   vision   use   cases

Azure's AutoML is integrated with ML pipelines and can be extended via Python SDK:

```
from azureml.train.automl import AutoMLConfig

automl_config = AutoMLConfig(
    task='classification',
    training_data=dataset,
    label_column_name='target',
    enable_early_stopping=True,
    primary_metric='accuracy',
    experiment_timeout_minutes=60
)
```

This makes it easier to automate experimentation, selection, and deployment of high-quality models.

---

7. Responsible AI Enhancements

As AI capabilities grow, Azure doubles down on responsible AI:

- **Responsible AI Dashboard** now includes counterfactual explanations and error analysis

- **Fairlearn and InterpretML** integrated directly into Azure ML pipelines

- **Azure AI Content Safety** for flagging harmful, biased, or sensitive outputs

Upcoming enhancements include real-time fairness auditing and sandboxed testing environments for high-risk models (e.g., healthcare or finance).

8. Real-Time AI and Edge Inference

With the growth of IoT and 5G, edge AI is gaining prominence. Azure supports:

- **Azure IoT Edge**: Deploy models to local gateways and devices

- **ONNX Runtime on Edge**: Lightweight, fast inference

- **Azure Percept Studio**: Preconfigured edge AI hardware and development tools

- **Azure Stack Edge**: On-premises appliances with GPU acceleration

Use cases include:

- Predictive maintenance in manufacturing

- Video analytics for smart cities

- Local anomaly detection in energy networks

9. Integration with Industry Workloads

Azure continues to develop AI solutions targeted at specific industries:

- **Healthcare**: Azure Health Bot, BioGPT, and medical imaging AI

- **Finance**: Fraud detection, document automation, risk modeling

- **Retail**: Demand forecasting, virtual assistants, dynamic pricing

- **Education**: Personalized learning assistants and AI tutors

Azure's industry clouds offer prebuilt APIs, data models, and security blueprints to accelerate adoption.

10. Quantum-Inspired and Neuromorphic AI

Looking further ahead, Microsoft is investing in **quantum-inspired optimization** and **neuromorphic computing**:

- **Azure Quantum**: Provides quantum optimization solvers usable for AI workloads

- **Project Brainwave**: Low-latency, FPGA-based inference

- **Spiking Neural Networks (SNNs)**: Research into energy-efficient AI

These innovations are paving the way for the next era of AI computation that goes beyond current silicon and software paradigms.

Summary

Azure's AI future is bold, expansive, and deeply integrated across tools, services, and domains. From generative AI and foundation models to autonomous agents and edge intelligence, Microsoft is building a cohesive ecosystem that empowers every organization to harness the transformative power of AI.

By staying at the forefront of these trends and leveraging Azure's innovation pipeline, developers and enterprises alike can build solutions that are not only intelligent—but also adaptable, responsible, and future-ready.

In the following sections, we'll examine how to prepare for this future through quantum and edge computing strategies, and how to keep learning and evolving as Azure's AI landscape continues to accelerate.

Preparing for Quantum and Edge AI

As we enter the next phase of computing, two frontiers stand out as pivotal to the advancement of artificial intelligence: **quantum computing** and **edge AI**. Each represents a radical shift in how we process data and solve complex problems. Quantum AI holds the potential to accelerate computations previously deemed intractable, while edge AI pushes intelligence closer to where data is generated—enabling low-latency, real-time insights in bandwidth-constrained or disconnected environments.

Microsoft Azure is uniquely positioned to lead in both domains. Azure Quantum provides a platform to begin building quantum-inspired solutions today, while Azure's edge offerings—

spanning IoT Edge, Azure Stack Edge, and ONNX Runtime—empower developers to deploy AI across diverse environments. In this section, we'll examine how to prepare your AI systems, teams, and strategies to harness these technologies as they mature.

Understanding Quantum AI

Quantum computing harnesses the principles of quantum mechanics—superposition, entanglement, and interference—to solve problems that are intractable for classical computers. Instead of binary bits (0 or 1), quantum bits or **qubits** can exist in multiple states simultaneously, enabling exponential computational space.

Quantum computing is particularly promising in areas such as:

- **Combinatorial optimization** (e.g., supply chain routing, portfolio optimization)

- **Molecular simulation** (e.g., drug discovery, materials science)

- **Machine learning** (e.g., kernel methods, data sampling, quantum-enhanced feature spaces)

Azure Quantum Overview

Azure Quantum is a **cloud-based platform for quantum computing** that provides:

- Access to quantum hardware (IonQ, Quantinuum, Rigetti, QCI)

- **Quantum simulators** for local or cloud-based development

- **Quantum-inspired optimization (QIO)** solvers for near-term use cases

- Integration with **Q#**, Microsoft's domain-specific quantum language

- SDKs in Python and .NET

Getting Started with Azure Quantum

1. Create a **Quantum Workspace** in Azure Portal.

2. Install the **qsharp** and **azure-quantum** Python packages.

3. Start coding with quantum circuits or optimization problems.

Example: Solving a constrained optimization problem

```
from azure.quantum.optimization import Problem, Term
from azure.quantum.optimization import ParallelTempering
from azure.quantum import Workspace

workspace = Workspace(
    subscription_id="your-subscription",
    resource_group="quantum-rg",
    name="quantum-workspace"
)

problem = Problem(name="Scheduling", problem_type="pubo")
problem.add_terms([Term(w=1, indices=[0, 1])])  # Simple example

solver = ParallelTempering(workspace)
result = solver.optimize(problem)
print(result)
```

This approach allows organizations to **harness quantum-inspired algorithms** on classical infrastructure while laying the groundwork for true quantum readiness.

Preparing for Edge AI

Edge AI refers to the deployment of AI models on devices at or near the data source rather than in centralized cloud servers. These devices range from IoT sensors and industrial equipment to mobile phones and autonomous vehicles.

Why Edge AI?

- **Low Latency**: Decisions need to be made instantly (e.g., in a self-driving car).

- **Bandwidth Efficiency**: Reduces the need to send large datasets to the cloud.

- **Data Privacy**: Sensitive data remains local (e.g., in healthcare or defense).

- **Offline Functionality**: Critical in remote areas or during network outages.

Azure's edge capabilities are powered by a wide range of tools:

- **Azure IoT Edge**: Framework to deploy containers to edge devices.

- **Azure Stack Edge**: Hardware appliance with built-in GPU acceleration.

- **ONNX Runtime**: High-performance inference engine optimized for CPUs, GPUs, and even FPGAs.

- **Azure Percept**: AI development platform for computer vision at the edge.

Building Edge AI Solutions with Azure

Step 1: Train Model in Azure ML

Use Azure Machine Learning Studio or SDK to train a model:

```
from sklearn.linear_model import LogisticRegression
from joblib import dump

model = LogisticRegression()
model.fit(X_train, y_train)
dump(model, "model.joblib")
```

Export the model to **ONNX format** for cross-platform deployment:

```
import onnxmltools
onnx_model              =                 onnxmltools.convert_sklearn(model,
initial_types=[("input", FloatTensorType([None, 4]))])
onnxmltools.utils.save_model(onnx_model, "model.onnx")
```

Step 2: Deploy with Azure IoT Edge

Package the model into a container module:

1. Create a Dockerfile with ONNX Runtime and model code.

2. Deploy the container as an IoT Edge module via the Azure IoT Hub.

```
az iot edge set-modules \
  --device-id edge-device-001 \
  --hub-name my-iothub \
  --content deployment.json
```

This enables edge devices to perform real-time inference with minimal latency.

Edge-Cloud Collaboration Patterns

Modern AI workloads often use a hybrid architecture where the edge and cloud collaborate:

- **Preprocessing at the edge,** full analytics in the cloud.

- **Filtering or summarizing data** before sending.

- **Model inference at the edge,** with **training in the cloud.**

- **Retraining and update distribution** via Azure IoT Hub.

This strategy balances performance, cost, and compliance requirements.

Challenges and Best Practices

Quantum AI Challenges:

- Current quantum hardware is noisy and limited in scale.

- Requires new skills in quantum algorithms and Q#.

- Best suited today for optimization and simulation, not general-purpose AI.

Edge AI Challenges:

- Device heterogeneity (ARM, x86, FPGA, GPU).

- Limited resources (battery, memory, CPU).

- Update management and monitoring at scale.

Best Practices:

Area	Recommendation
Model Optimization	Use quantization, pruning, and ONNX for efficient edge inference

Network Planning	Design for intermittent connectivity
Device Management	Use Azure IoT Hub + Device Update
Security	Encrypt models, authenticate modules, isolate workloads
Quantum Readiness	Start with QIO solvers for practical benefits today
Workforce Enablement	Train teams in quantum fundamentals and edge engineering

Future Outlook

1. **Quantum Supremacy for ML**: Algorithms like QSVM, quantum annealing, and quantum neural networks will transition from theoretical to practical.

2. **Federated and Swarm AI**: Edge devices will learn collaboratively while preserving data locality.

3. **Neuromorphic Hardware**: Brain-like processors (e.g., Intel Loihi) will power ultra-efficient AI at the edge.

4. **Edge-to-Edge Learning**: Models retrain using peer edge devices without cloud involvement.

Azure's vision is to **create a continuum of intelligence**—where models can be trained, tuned, deployed, and evolved across cloud, edge, and quantum environments without boundaries.

Summary

Preparing for quantum and edge AI is not about immediate adoption, but about **building readiness** for the next frontier of intelligent systems. With Azure's growing portfolio of services—from Azure Quantum to IoT Edge and ONNX Runtime—developers and enterprises are empowered to build adaptive, resilient, and future-proof AI solutions.

The convergence of cloud-scale training, edge-level inference, and quantum-enhanced reasoning will define the next decade of AI. Organizations that invest today in skills, architecture, and experimentation will be best positioned to lead tomorrow's innovations.

Next, we'll explore how to keep pace with the rapidly evolving Azure AI landscape through continuous learning, community engagement, and staying aligned with best practices and product updates.

Continuous Learning and Staying Updated

Artificial Intelligence is a dynamic field, and when combined with a fast-evolving platform like Microsoft Azure, staying current becomes both a challenge and a necessity. New services, features, SDKs, models, and best practices are released frequently. The tools and frameworks used to build AI solutions today may evolve significantly within months, affecting everything from code deployment to model governance.

This section provides a comprehensive guide to continuous learning strategies and resources tailored to AI practitioners working in the Azure ecosystem. Whether you're a data scientist, machine learning engineer, developer, or architect, these practices will help you stay sharp, relevant, and proactive in your AI career.

The Importance of Continuous Learning in Azure AI

Azure AI evolves across several axes simultaneously:

- **New services and APIs** (e.g., Azure OpenAI, Prompt Flow, AI Content Safety)

- **Framework updates** (e.g., Azure Machine Learning SDK, ONNX Runtime)

- **Platform integration changes** (e.g., Azure DevOps, GitHub Actions, Arc)

- **Model deployment paradigms** (e.g., serverless, hybrid, AKS)

- **Security and compliance policies** (e.g., Responsible AI, region-specific regulations)

Failing to adapt to these changes can result in outdated architectures, inefficient resource usage, or even compliance risks.

Core Learning Areas for AI on Azure

1. **Platform Fundamentals**

   - Azure Resource Management
   - Identity and access control (RBAC, Azure AD)
   - Networking and security (VNets, Private Endpoints)

2. **Data Engineering**

- o Azure Data Factory, Synapse Analytics, Databricks
- o Data Lake Gen2 and Structured Streaming

3. **Machine** **Learning**

- o Azure Machine Learning Studio + SDK (Python)
- o Automated ML, custom model training, drift monitoring
- o Deployment options: real-time, batch, managed endpoints

4. **Cognitive** **Services**

- o Vision, Speech, Language APIs
- o Azure OpenAI for generative tasks

5. **DevOps** **+** **MLOps**

- o Azure DevOps, GitHub Actions
- o CI/CD pipelines for models
- o Model versioning and rollback

6. **Compliance** **and** **Responsible** **AI**

- o Model explainability
- o Bias and fairness
- o GDPR, HIPAA, and ISO compliance controls

Microsoft Learning Platforms

Microsoft offers structured learning through multiple platforms:

Microsoft Learn

An official and interactive learning platform with guided modules and real-time sandbox environments.

Recommended Learning Paths:

- *Build and operationalize machine learning solutions with Azure Machine Learning*

- *Create intelligent apps with Azure AI services*

- *Design and implement an Azure AI solution (AI-102 Exam Prep)*

Each module includes real labs where users interact directly with Azure services.

https://learn.microsoft.com/training/paths/create-machine-learning-models-azure/

Microsoft Certifications

Structured certifications help validate expertise and are often valued by employers.

- **AI-900**: Azure AI Fundamentals

- **DP-100**: Designing and Implementing an Azure Data Science Solution

- **AI-102**: Designing and Implementing an Azure AI Solution

- **AZ-305**: Designing Azure Infrastructure Solutions

Community-Driven Resources

GitHub Repositories

Explore open-source projects and reference architectures:

- Microsoft's official repos:

  o azure/azureml-examples

  o microsoft/azure-openai-samples

  o microsoft/semantic-kernel

- Community-contributed:

  o microsoft/AI-For-Beginners

  o microsoft/ML-For-Beginners

Use GitHub notifications or tools like **GitHub Stars** to track updates to your favorite repos.

Blogs and Newsletters

- **Azure AI Blog**: Weekly announcements and feature breakdowns
- **Tech Community AI**: Discussions, demos, and use case stories
- **Data Science Dojo, Towards Data Science**: Often include Azure ML use cases

Subscribe to newsletters such as:

- *Azure* *Weekly*
- *The* *Batch* *(by* *deeplearning.ai)*
- *Microsoft* *Source*

Conferences, Meetups, and Online Events

Attend regular events to stay in tune with trends and network with peers.

Major Conferences:

- **Microsoft Build**: Developer-centric, includes AI announcements
- **Microsoft Ignite**: Enterprise-grade AI infrastructure and strategy
- **Azure Open Source Day**: Hands-on technical deep-dives

Specialized Summits:

- **AI for Good Summit**
- **MLConf**
- **Responsible AI Forum**

Many of these are available as virtual events with free access to recordings.

Staying Ahead with Product Announcements

Stay subscribed to Microsoft product roadmaps and RSS feeds:

- Azure Updates: https://azure.microsoft.com/updates/

- Azure AI Release Notes

- Cognitive Services and OpenAI changelogs

- Azure SDK Release Announcements on GitHub

Use automation tools like **IFTTT, Zapier**, or **Microsoft Power Automate** to get alerts when specific services update.

Experimentation as a Learning Tool

The best way to learn Azure AI is to **build continuously**.

Challenge Ideas:

- Build an AI-powered résumé analyzer using Azure Form Recognizer + GPT

- Deploy a custom image classifier to Raspberry Pi with IoT Edge

- Create a multi-language support bot using Translator + LUIS + Power Virtual Agents

- Use Azure ML pipelines to automate dataset versioning and retraining

- Connect Azure Cognitive Search with OpenAI for a semantic RAG solution

Keep a repo or digital portfolio of all experiments—this is useful for learning, showcasing, and reviewing your own growth.

Staying Collaborative

- **Join AI and ML Slack groups or Discord communities**

- **Answer or post on Stack Overflow and Microsoft Q&A**

- **Contribute to open-source ML projects or Azure feedback forums**

Collaboration leads to better learning outcomes and ensures your knowledge aligns with industry needs.

Periodic Skill Reviews and Refreshes

At least once every 6 months:

- Revisit your AI stack and Azure service usage
- Re-evaluate your cost, latency, and scaling patterns
- Update CI/CD and security policies
- Check for deprecated APIs or SDK changes
- Reread Microsoft's Responsible AI Standard updates

Automate these checks as part of a **tech debt review** or **architecture governance process**.

Summary

In the fast-paced world of Azure AI, continuous learning is not optional—it's a professional necessity. By combining structured learning, experimentation, community engagement, and real-time awareness of platform changes, you can future-proof your skills and maintain your edge as an AI practitioner.

Azure provides an evolving ecosystem that rewards curiosity and initiative. From foundational AI to cutting-edge quantum and edge computing, staying engaged with the platform's innovations ensures your solutions are efficient, secure, and aligned with global standards.

In the next chapter, the appendices will provide additional resources: glossaries, reference guides, sample projects, and code snippets to reinforce everything you've learned throughout this book.

Chapter 11: APPENDICES

Glossary of Terms

The language of artificial intelligence and cloud computing can be dense, especially when embedded within the ever-expanding landscape of the Azure ecosystem. To navigate this complex environment with confidence, it's critical to develop fluency in key terms and concepts. This glossary aims to demystify essential vocabulary spanning Azure services, machine learning methodologies, infrastructure components, and responsible AI principles. Whether you're a beginner or revisiting fundamentals, the following definitions will help ground your understanding and accelerate your learning journey.

A

AI   **(Artificial**   **Intelligence)**
A branch of computer science focused on building systems capable of performing tasks that normally require human intelligence—such as perception, reasoning, learning, and decision-making.

AKS   **(Azure**   **Kubernetes**   **Service)**
A managed Kubernetes container orchestration service used to deploy, manage, and scale containerized applications—including AI models.

API   **(Application**   **Programming**   **Interface)**
A defined set of rules that allows different software components to communicate. Azure offers numerous APIs for AI, such as Cognitive Services and Azure OpenAI endpoints.

AutoML   **(Automated**   **Machine**   **Learning)**
A feature in Azure Machine Learning that automates the process of training, selecting, and tuning models, making machine learning accessible to non-experts.

B

Batch   **Inference**
Processing multiple predictions at once, often using a scheduled pipeline. Azure ML supports batch endpoints for cost-effective inference at scale.

Blob   **Storage**
An object storage solution from Azure used to store unstructured data like images, videos, documents, and model artifacts.

Bring   Your   Own   Model   (BYOM)
The process of importing and deploying a custom-trained model into Azure ML or other Azure AI services, as opposed to using prebuilt models.

C

CLI   (Command-Line   Interface)
A text-based interface for interacting with Azure services. Azure CLI allows you to manage resources, train models, deploy services, and more via command line.

Cognitive   Services
A suite of prebuilt AI APIs that provide capabilities in vision, speech, language, decision-making, and search.

Container   Registry   (ACR)
Azure Container Registry allows you to build, store, and manage container images for use in AKS or IoT Edge deployments.

Compute   Target
The Azure resource where your ML jobs run. Can be a local machine, a remote VM, or a cluster managed by Azure ML.

D

Data   Drift
A change in the input data that can lead to decreased model performance over time. Azure ML offers tools to detect and manage data drift.

Data   Factory   (ADF)
A data integration service that helps build ETL and ELT pipelines for processing data across on-prem and cloud systems.

Data   Lake   Storage   Gen2
An optimized Azure storage service designed for big data analytics, offering hierarchical namespaces, high throughput, and integration with tools like Synapse and Databricks.

Deployment   Endpoint
An API endpoint where a trained machine learning model is hosted to receive prediction requests.

E

Edge AI
The deployment of AI models on local devices (e.g., IoT sensors, cameras) to perform inference without relying on continuous internet connectivity.

ETL **(Extract,** **Transform,** **Load)**
A process used in data engineering to move and prepare data for analytics and machine learning.

Experiment
In Azure ML, an experiment is a grouping of model training runs used to track performance and versioning.

F

Fairness **(Responsible** **AI)**
A principle ensuring that AI systems do not discriminate based on protected characteristics such as race, gender, or age. Azure provides toolkits like Fairlearn for measuring and mitigating bias.

Feature **Store**
A centralized repository for storing and sharing machine learning features for reuse across models and teams.

G

GPU **(Graphics** **Processing** **Unit)**
A specialized processor designed for high-performance computations. Used extensively in deep learning model training and inference.

GitHub **Actions**
A CI/CD platform tightly integrated with Azure services, used to automate testing, training, and deployment workflows.

H

Hyperparameter **Tuning**
The process of optimizing model parameters that are not learned from data but affect training, such as learning rate or number of estimators.

Hybrid **Cloud**
A computing environment combining on-premises infrastructure, private cloud services, and public cloud—made manageable via solutions like Azure Arc.

I

Inference
The process of applying a trained machine learning model to new data to generate predictions.

Interpreter
A tool or method used to explain how a model arrives at its decisions. Examples include SHAP values and counterfactual explanations.

J

Jupyter **Notebooks**
Interactive documents that allow users to write and execute code in Python (and other languages) alongside markdown notes. Fully supported within Azure ML Studio.

K

Kubernetes
An open-source platform for automating deployment, scaling, and management of containerized applications. Managed by Azure as AKS.

Kusto **Query** **Language** **(KQL)**
A powerful query language used in Azure Monitor and Log Analytics for querying structured logs and telemetry.

L

Large **Language** **Model** **(LLM)**
A type of deep learning model trained on massive text corpora to understand and generate human-like text. Azure offers access to OpenAI's LLMs through managed APIs.

Lifecycle **Management**
The process of managing the end-to-end lifecycle of machine learning models, including development, deployment, monitoring, and retirement.

M

Managed   **Identity**
An automatically managed identity in Azure Active Directory used to authenticate to services that support Azure AD authentication.

Model   **Registry**
A centralized store for versioned models, used to track, manage, and promote models through stages (e.g., dev, test, production).

MLOps
Machine Learning Operations: a set of practices to unify ML system development and deployment (DevOps for ML).

N

Notebook   **VM**
A preconfigured virtual machine environment in Azure ML for running Jupyter notebooks, useful for experimentation and prototyping.

Neural   **Network**
A type of model in deep learning, inspired by biological neural systems, consisting of layers of interconnected nodes or "neurons."

O

ONNX   **(Open**   **Neural**   **Network**   **Exchange)**
A standard format for representing ML models, supported across frameworks like PyTorch, TensorFlow, and Azure ML. Optimized for inference with ONNX Runtime.

OpenAI
A research organization whose models (e.g., GPT, Codex) are available on Azure through the Azure OpenAI Service.

P

Pipeline
A sequence of data processing and model training steps, automated using Azure ML pipelines or Data Factory workflows.

Prompt   **Engineering**
The practice of designing effective inputs ("prompts") for large language models to produce desired outputs.

Q

Quantum-Inspired Optimization (QIO)
Classical algorithms that simulate the advantages of quantum systems for solving optimization problems. Offered in Azure Quantum.

R

RAG (Retrieval-Augmented Generation)
An architecture that combines large language models with search capabilities to retrieve relevant documents before generating answers. Supported with Azure OpenAI + Cognitive Search.

Responsible AI
A framework encompassing fairness, reliability, transparency, and privacy. Azure embeds these principles across its AI tooling.

S

Scoring Script
A Python script used during deployment to define how incoming data is processed and how predictions are returned.

Synapse Analytics
An Azure analytics service that integrates big data and data warehousing capabilities with serverless and provisioned compute.

T

TensorFlow
An open-source machine learning framework widely used for training and deploying deep learning models. Azure ML supports training and deployment for TensorFlow models.

Trigger
In Azure Functions or Logic Apps, a condition that initiates execution (e.g., a new file in storage or a REST call).

U

Unstructured **Data**
Data that does not have a predefined format, such as text, images, audio, or video. Common in AI workloads and stored in Azure Blob Storage or Data Lake.

V

Virtual **Network** **(VNet)**
An Azure networking construct that enables secure communication between Azure resources, on-premises environments, and the internet.

Versioning
Tracking different iterations of models, datasets, and experiments to ensure reproducibility and manage change.

W

Workspace **(Azure** **ML)**
The foundational resource in Azure Machine Learning where all assets—models, datasets, experiments, endpoints—are organized and managed.

Workload
A set of computing tasks, such as training a model, running a pipeline, or performing batch scoring.

X

XAI **(Explainable** **AI)**
A set of techniques and tools aimed at making AI decisions understandable to humans, crucial for building trust in AI systems.

Y

YAML **(YAML** **Ain't** **Markup** **Language)**
A human-readable configuration language used to define Azure pipelines, Kubernetes deployments, and ML experiments.

Z

Zero   Trust   Architecture

A security model that assumes breach and verifies each request as though it originates from an open network—relevant to securing AI systems and data pipelines in the cloud.

Summary

This glossary serves as your quick-reference companion throughout the book and your future AI projects on Azure. Familiarity with these terms will enhance your understanding of architectural decisions, coding patterns, deployment workflows, and compliance considerations. You're encouraged to revisit this glossary often as you progress through advanced topics and hands-on implementation.

In the next appendix, you'll find a curated list of resources for deepening your skills, staying up to date with Azure AI developments, and engaging with the wider AI community.

Resources for Further Learning

To stay current, advance your skills, and build confidence in developing AI solutions using Azure, continuous learning is vital. Fortunately, Microsoft and the broader AI community offer an expansive ecosystem of high-quality resources—from documentation and tutorials to certifications, developer tools, and expert communities. Whether you're a student, a professional developer, a data scientist, or an architect, the following curated resources will empower you to deepen your knowledge and expand your capabilities with Azure AI.

This section compiles the most reliable and frequently updated learning resources, organized into categories for easy reference. It also includes strategies for effective learning, recommendations for building a personal study roadmap, and suggestions for engaging with industry-leading experts and communities.

Microsoft Learn

Microsoft Learn is the most official and comprehensive starting point for structured Azure training.

Key features:

- Interactive modules and learning paths with free sandboxes.

- Role-based paths (developer, data scientist, solutions architect).

- Exam preparation material for certifications.

- Progress tracking and gamification (XP points, trophies).

Recommended Azure AI Paths:

- *Create machine learning models*

- *Build intelligent apps with Azure AI services*

- *Automate ML with Azure Machine Learning*

- *Build computer vision solutions*

- *Design Azure AI solutions (AI-102)*

Each module combines theoretical knowledge, interactive exercises, and assessments to reinforce learning.

Microsoft Certification Paths

Certifications validate your skills and demonstrate expertise to employers and clients. Microsoft offers several Azure certifications specifically focused on AI and data science:

- **AI-900: Azure AI Fundamentals**
  Great for non-technical or beginner roles looking to understand Azure AI concepts.

- **DP-100: Designing and Implementing a Data Science Solution on Azure**
  Targeted at data scientists building and deploying models using Azure Machine Learning.

- **AI-102: Designing and Implementing an Azure AI Solution**
  Focused on developers implementing AI workloads using Cognitive Services and Bot Framework.

- **AZ-305 / AZ-400** (Optional but useful):
  For cloud architects and DevOps engineers involved in deploying AI workloads at scale.

Each certification includes:

- Free or paid self-study paths on Microsoft Learn.

- Practice exams from MeasureUp and Whizlabs.

- Exam vouchers and discounts for students or via events like Microsoft Build.

Azure AI Documentation

The **Azure AI documentation** portal is the single most authoritative reference for all Azure AI services.

Documentation categories:

- Azure Machine Learning SDK and CLI
- Azure OpenAI Service
- Language, Vision, Speech, and Decision APIs
- Responsible AI tooling
- Deployment and MLOps guides

Each service page includes:

- Overview
- Quickstarts
- How-to guides
- API references
- Tutorials and sample notebooks

GitHub Repositories and Open Source Projects

Microsoft and the community maintain a vast collection of Azure AI code samples, tools, and templates on GitHub.

Notable Repos:

- azure/azureml-examples – End-to-end Azure ML samples (training, deployment, pipelines).

- microsoft/semantic-kernel – SDK for building AI agents with OpenAI, search, and memory.

- microsoft/azure-openai-samples – Code templates for chatbots, summarizers, and RAG pipelines.

- microsoft/AI-For-Beginners – Foundational AI course with Jupyter Notebooks.

- microsoft/Responsible-AI-Toolbox – Tools for explainability, fairness, error analysis.

Use GitHub Discussions, Issues, and Stars to interact with project maintainers and track evolving feature sets.

Community and Forums

Engaging with a community accelerates learning, fosters collaboration, and helps resolve blockers faster.

Microsoft Communities:

- Microsoft Tech Community – Blogs, events, AMAs.

- Azure Q&A – Official question-answering site for Azure services.

- Microsoft Reactor – Free technical workshops and events.

- Microsoft AI Discord – Real-time discussion and peer support.

Third-Party Communities:

- Stack Overflow (azure-machine-learning, azure-openai)

- Reddit (e.g., r/AZURE, r/MachineLearning)

- Data Science Slack, Hugging Face community forums

- Meetup.com groups in major cities

YouTube and Video Learning

Microsoft AI YouTube Channels:

- Microsoft Azure

- AI Show

- Build / Ignite Keynotes

Curated Playlists:

- Building and operationalizing ML with Azure
- Azure AI services overview
- OpenAI integration demos
- Cognitive Search and Language Studio

Newsletters, Blogs, and Podcasts

Newsletters:

- *Azure* *Weekly*
- *The* *Batch* by DeepLearning.AI
- *Import* *AI* by Jack Clark
- *Data* *Elixir* — Curated data science articles

Blogs:

- Azure AI Blog
- Medium: Towards Data Science
- Microsoft DevBlogs for Python, ML, and DevOps

Podcasts:

- *AI* *in* *Business* (Dan Faggella)
- *The* *AI* *Alignment* *Podcast*
- *Data* *Skeptic*
- *AI* *Today* *Podcast*

AI Sandbox and Lab Environments

Azure **Free** **Trial**
https://azure.microsoft.com/free

- $200 credit for 30 days

- Access to most AI services

- Always-free tier (e.g., Azure Functions, Cosmos DB)

Cloud **Skills** **Challenge**
Often available during Microsoft events; complete challenges to win certifications, badges, or gear.

AI Labs

- AI Demos

- Cognitive Services Labs

- Azure AI Gallery — Legacy but still valuable for visual learners.

Build Your Personal Learning Plan

To avoid overwhelm and stay focused, consider creating a custom roadmap.

Step **1:** **Define** **your** **goal**
Examples:

- Become Azure AI certified in 90 days

- Build an intelligent chatbot for customer support

- Deploy an ML model to AKS with CI/CD

Step 2: Choose your format

- Visual learner: Use YouTube, Pluralsight, and Labs

- Code-first learner: Focus on GitHub and Jupyter Notebooks

- Theoretical learner: Microsoft Learn, whitepapers, Coursera

Step 3: Schedule time

- 30 mins daily or 3 hours/week

- Join a study group or challenge cohort

Step 4: Track Progress

Use Trello, Notion, or a GitHub repo to document what you've learned, tested, and built.

Summary

Azure's AI ecosystem is as expansive as it is empowering—but only if you commit to continuous learning. This curated collection of learning resources, community platforms, and study frameworks will help you navigate your journey from beginner to advanced practitioner.

Whether your next milestone is deploying your first AI model, passing a certification exam, or architecting a multi-service AI platform, these tools will support your development every step of the way. Keep experimenting, keep learning, and above all, stay connected to the incredible global community building the future of AI on Azure.

Sample Projects and Code Snippets

Hands-on experience is critical to mastering AI development on Azure. While theoretical knowledge and documentation are essential, nothing accelerates learning faster than building real applications. This section provides a curated collection of sample projects and reusable code snippets that illustrate how to leverage Azure's AI capabilities in practical, end-to-end scenarios.

These projects range from beginner-friendly to advanced and span common domains like natural language processing (NLP), computer vision, conversational AI, and real-time analytics. Each example includes implementation tips, Azure services used, and code snippets in Python, JavaScript, or CLI to help you get started immediately.

1. Sentiment Analysis Web App

Goal: Create a web-based tool that uses Azure Cognitive Services to detect sentiment from user input.

Azure Services:

- Azure Text Analytics API (Sentiment)

- Azure App Service (Hosting)

- Azure Functions (API Layer)

Key Code Snippet (Python with Flask + Azure SDK):

```python
from azure.ai.textanalytics import TextAnalyticsClient
from azure.core.credentials import AzureKeyCredential
from flask import Flask, request, jsonify

key = "YOUR_API_KEY"
endpoint = "https://YOUR-RESOURCE.cognitiveservices.azure.com/"

client = TextAnalyticsClient(endpoint=endpoint,
credential=AzureKeyCredential(key))
app = Flask(__name__)

@app.route("/analyze", methods=["POST"])
def analyze_sentiment():
    text = request.json["text"]
    response = client.analyze_sentiment([text])[0]
    return jsonify({
        "sentiment": response.sentiment,
        "scores": response.confidence_scores.__dict__
    })
```

Deploy this using Azure App Service or as a serverless Azure Function.

---

2. Image Classification with Custom Vision

Goal: Train a custom image classifier to identify categories (e.g., fruits, products, wildlife).

Azure Services:

- Custom Vision Training and Prediction API
- Azure Storage (Blob for datasets)

Steps:

1. Upload labeled images to Blob Storage.

2. Create a project in Custom Vision.

3. Train your model and test it in the portal.

4. Export the model as a TensorFlow or ONNX file for deployment.

Python Prediction Snippet:

```
from azure.cognitiveservices.vision.customvision.prediction import
CustomVisionPredictionClient
from msrest.authentication import ApiKeyCredentials

credentials = ApiKeyCredentials(in_headers={"Prediction-key": "<your-
key>"})
predictor    =    CustomVisionPredictionClient("<your-endpoint>",
credentials)

with open("test-image.jpg", "rb") as image:
    results = predictor.classify_image("<project-id>", "<publish-
name>", image)

for prediction in results.predictions:
    print(f"{prediction.tag_name}: {prediction.probability:.2f}")
```

This project can also be deployed on mobile apps or edge devices.

---

3. Chatbot with Azure Bot Framework and LUIS

Goal: Build an intelligent FAQ bot that understands intent and entities.

Azure Services:

- LUIS (Language Understanding Intelligent Service)

- Azure Bot Service

- Azure App Service

Steps:

1. Create a bot using Bot Framework SDK (Node.js or Python).

2. Connect LUIS model for intent detection.

3. Define intents like GetHours, LocationQuery, ContactSupport.

4. Deploy on Azure App Service or integrate with Teams.

Dialog Sample (Node.js):

```javascript
const { LuisRecognizer } = require('botbuilder-ai');

const luisConfig = {
    applicationId: "<LUIS-ID>",
    endpointKey: "<LUIS-KEY>",
    endpoint: "<LUIS-ENDPOINT>"
};

const recognizer = new LuisRecognizer(luisConfig, {
    apiVersion: "v3"
}, true);

const intent = await recognizer.recognize(turnContext);
const topIntent = LuisRecognizer.topIntent(intent);

switch(topIntent) {
    case "GetHours":
        await context.sendActivity("We're open from 9 AM to 5 PM,
Monday through Friday.");
        break;
}
```

Bots can be extended with QnA Maker, Translator, or Speech services.

---

4. Predictive Maintenance with Azure ML

Goal: Predict equipment failure using time-series sensor data.

Azure Services:

- Azure   Machine   Learning

- Azure Blob Storage
- Azure Data Factory (ETL)

Workflow:

1. Collect telemetry from IoT sensors.
2. Store in Blob Storage.
3. Build a time-series classification model in Azure ML.
4. Deploy as a real-time endpoint.

Training Snippet (Python):

```python
from sklearn.ensemble import RandomForestClassifier
from azureml.core import Dataset

df = dataset.to_pandas_dataframe()
X = df.drop(columns="failure")
y = df["failure"]

model = RandomForestClassifier(n_estimators=100)
model.fit(X, y)

import joblib
joblib.dump(model, "rf_model.pkl")
```

Deploy with `inference_config` and `deployment_config` using Azure ML SDK.

---

5. Real-Time Object Detection on Edge Device

Goal: Deploy an ONNX object detection model to a Raspberry Pi using Azure IoT Edge.

Azure Services:

- Azure IoT Hub
- Azure IoT Edge

- ONNX   Runtime

- Azure   Container   Registry

Edge Deployment Snippet (Docker):

```
FROM mcr.microsoft.com/onnxruntime/python

COPY yolov5.onnx /model/
COPY app.py /app/
CMD ["python", "/app/app.py"]
```

Build and push image to ACR, then deploy using `deployment.json` via Azure CLI.

---

6. Retrieval-Augmented Generation (RAG) with Azure OpenAI and Cognitive Search

Goal: Build an enterprise knowledge assistant that answers questions from internal documents.

Azure Services:

- Azure   Cognitive   Search

- Azure   OpenAI   (GPT-4)

- Azure   Blob   Storage   (for   PDFs,   DOCX,   etc.)

- Azure   Function   App   (API   endpoint)

Example Prompt Flow (Python):

```
from openai import AzureOpenAI
from azure.search.documents import SearchClient

search_client = SearchClient(endpoint, index_name, credential)
results = search_client.search("How do I submit an expense report?")
passages = "\n".join([doc["content"] for doc in results])

prompt = f"""
You are a helpful assistant. Based on the following context, answer
the question:
```

```
Context: {passages}
Question: How do I submit an expense report?
"""

response = openai.ChatCompletion.create(
    engine="gpt-4",
    messages=[{"role": "user", "content": prompt}]
)
print(response.choices[0].message["content"])
```

This is one of the most impactful use cases for knowledge management in the enterprise.

---

7. Serverless ML Inference with Azure Functions

Goal: Trigger real-time predictions using a trained model deployed in a lightweight serverless endpoint.

Azure Services:

- Azure Functions (Python)

- Azure ML Model Registry

- Azure Blob Storage

Sample Function Code:

```
import joblib
import json
import azure.functions as func

model = joblib.load("model.pkl")

def main(req: func.HttpRequest) -> func.HttpResponse:
    input_data = json.loads(req.get_body())
    prediction = model.predict([input_data["features"]])
    return                func.HttpResponse(json.dumps({"result":
int(prediction[0])}))
```

Deploy using VS Code + Azure Functions extension or the Azure CLI.

Summary

These projects demonstrate how Azure's AI services can be composed into powerful, real-world applications that span industries and use cases. Whether you're building with prebuilt APIs like Cognitive Services or training your own models in Azure ML, these samples offer a concrete starting point to expand your skills.

You're encouraged to customize, scale, and share these projects. Use GitHub for versioning, integrate with CI/CD using Azure DevOps or GitHub Actions, and consider extending each project with responsible AI tools for fairness and transparency.

In the following appendix sections, we'll provide quick-reference API documentation and address frequently asked questions to support your development and troubleshooting efforts.

API Reference Guide

APIs are the cornerstone of scalable, modular AI solutions in the Azure ecosystem. Whether you're consuming prebuilt AI capabilities through Azure Cognitive Services, interacting with Azure Machine Learning endpoints, or integrating models via the Azure OpenAI service, understanding API structures and patterns is essential. This section provides a comprehensive reference guide to the most relevant AI-related APIs in Azure.

We will explore endpoint structures, authentication patterns, payload formats, rate limits, best practices, and example usages for key AI services. The focus is on real-world utility: you'll find sample API calls, configuration options, and integration tips for languages like Python, JavaScript, and CLI tools.

1. Azure OpenAI API

Base **Endpoint:**

```
https://<your-resource-
name>.openai.azure.com/openai/deployments/<deployment-
name>/completions?api-version=2023-03-15-preview
```

Authentication:
Use API keys or Azure Active Directory (recommended for enterprise apps).

Sample Request (Python):

```python
import openai

openai.api_type = "azure"
openai.api_key = "your-key"
```

```
openai.api_base = "https://your-resource.openai.azure.com/"
openai.api_version = "2023-03-15-preview"

response = openai.ChatCompletion.create(
    engine="gpt-4",
    messages=[
        {"role": "system", "content": "You are a helpful assistant."},
        {"role": "user", "content": "What is Azure OpenAI?"}
    ]
)
print(response["choices"][0]["message"]["content"])
```

Parameters:

- `temperature:` 0.0–1.0 (controls creativity)

- `max_tokens:` limit response length

- `top_p:` nucleus sampling

- `stop:` sequence(s) to stop on

Rate Limits:

- Determined by deployment type (e.g., GPT-4 throughput is lower than GPT-3.5)

- Use Azure Quota API to check and request increases

---

2. Azure Cognitive Services

Text Analytics (Sentiment, Key Phrases, Language Detection)

Endpoint:

```
https://<resource>.cognitiveservices.azure.com/text/analytics/v3.1/s
entiment
```

Authentication:
 Header: `Ocp-Apim-Subscription-Key: <key>`

Request Body:

```json
{
  "documents": [
    {
      "id": "1",
      "language": "en",
      "text": "I love using Azure AI tools!"
    }
  ]
}
```

Sample Python Call:

```python
import requests

headers = {
    "Ocp-Apim-Subscription-Key": "your-key",
    "Content-Type": "application/json"
}
endpoint = "https://your-resource.cognitiveservices.azure.com/text/analytics/v3.1/sentiment"

response = requests.post(endpoint, headers=headers, json={
    "documents": [{"id": "1", "text": "Azure is amazing!", "language": "en"}]
})
print(response.json())
```

Output Format:

```json
{
  "documents": [
    {
      "id": "1",
      "sentiment": "positive",
      "confidenceScores": {
        "positive": 0.98,
        "neutral": 0.02,
        "negative": 0.0
      }
    }
  ]
```

```
}
```

Computer Vision (OCR, Tags, Analysis)

Endpoint:
```
https://<region>.api.cognitive.microsoft.com/vision/v3.2/analyze
```

Features:

- `visualFeatures`: Categories, Tags, Faces, Description, Objects

- `language`: en, es, etc.

- `details`: Celebrities, Landmarks

Example:

```
files = {'image': open('sample.jpg', 'rb')}
params = {'visualFeatures': 'Description,Tags'}
headers = {
    'Ocp-Apim-Subscription-Key': '<your-key>'
}
resp = requests.post(endpoint, headers=headers, params=params,
files=files)
print(resp.json())
```

3. Azure Machine Learning REST API

Used for deploying, invoking, and managing ML models.

Endpoint:

```
https://<region>.inference.ml.azure.com/score
```

Authentication:

- Bearer token via Azure AD
- Managed identity or Service Principal

Headers:

```
Authorization: Bearer <token>
Content-Type: application/json
azureml-model-deployment: <deployment-name>
```

Request Payload:

```
{
  "input_data": {
    "columns": ["feature1", "feature2"],
    "index": [0],
    "data": [[1.2, 3.4]]
  }
}
```

Sample Python Request:

```python
import requests

token = "your-AAD-access-token"
headers = {
    "Authorization": f"Bearer {token}",
    "Content-Type": "application/json",
    "azureml-model-deployment": "my-model"
}

data = {
    "input_data": {
        "columns": ["age", "income"],
        "index": [0],
        "data": [[32, 48000]]
    }
}

response =
requests.post("https://region.inference.ml.azure.com/score",
headers=headers, json=data)
print(response.json())
```

4. Azure Translator API

Endpoint:

```
https://api.cognitive.microsofttranslator.com/translate?api-
version=3.0&to=es
```

Headers:

```
Ocp-Apim-Subscription-Key: <key>
Content-Type: application/json
```

Sample Request:

```
body = [{"Text": "Hello, how are you?"}]
response = requests.post(endpoint, headers=headers, json=body)
print(response.json())
```

Response:

```
[
  {
    "translations": [
      {
        "text": "Hola, ¿cómo estás?",
        "to": "es"
      }
    ]
  }
]
```

5. Azure Form Recognizer API

Used for extracting structured data from receipts, invoices, and custom forms.

Endpoint:

```
https://<resource>.cognitiveservices.azure.com/formrecognizer/docume
ntModels/prebuilt-invoice:analyze?api-version=2023-07-31
```

Authentication: API Key or Azure AD

Steps:

1. Upload   document   to   Blob   Storage   or   use   file   stream.

2. Call the analyze API.

3. Poll `operation-location` until status is succeeded.

Sample Code:

```
headers = {
    "Ocp-Apim-Subscription-Key": key,
    "Content-Type": "application/pdf"
}
response      =      requests.post(endpoint,      headers=headers,
data=open("invoice.pdf", "rb"))
operation_url = response.headers["Operation-Location"]

# Poll status
result = requests.get(operation_url, headers={"Ocp-Apim-Subscription-
Key": key})
```

6. Azure Search + OpenAI (RAG)

Search API Endpoint:
```
https://<search-service>.search.windows.net/indexes/<index-
name>/docs/search?api-version=2021-04-30-Preview
```

Headers:

- `api-key:` Admin or query key

- `Content-Type:` application/json

Payload Example:

```
{
  "search": "How do I file an expense report?",
  "top": 5
}
```

Combine with OpenAI for retrieval-augmented generation.

Best Practices for Azure AI API Usage

Practice	Description
Use AAD authentication	Especially for production environments and role-based access
Implement retry logic	APIs may occasionally fail due to transient issues
Monitor quota usage	Azure Portal → Cognitive Services → Usage and Quotas
Secure API keys and tokens	Store in Azure Key Vault or environment variables
Handle versioning	Always specify the correct `api-version` in requests
Validate response schema	APIs may return nulls, errors, or partial results

Summary

This API reference guide provides essential documentation for working with Azure's most powerful AI tools. From OpenAI's language models to cognitive APIs for vision, speech, and documents, the ability to interact fluently with these endpoints is key to building modern intelligent applications.

Use this appendix as a quick lookup tool during development, prototyping, and integration. In the final appendix, we'll answer frequently asked questions that arise during the real-world use of these services.

Frequently Asked Questions

Building AI applications on Azure can raise a variety of technical, strategic, and operational questions. This FAQ compiles and answers the most commonly asked questions by developers, architects, and data scientists working with Azure AI services. These are grouped into categories to help you find relevant information quickly—from model deployment and cost management to responsible AI practices and real-time performance.

General AI on Azure

Q: What are the main differences between Azure Machine Learning and Azure Cognitive Services?

A:
Azure Machine Learning is a platform for developing, training, and deploying custom models, primarily used by data scientists and ML engineers. It offers high flexibility, control, and scalability.
Azure Cognitive Services provides prebuilt AI capabilities via simple APIs (e.g., vision, speech, language) and is ideal for developers who want to integrate AI quickly without building models from scratch.

Q: Can I integrate multiple Azure AI services into a single application?

A:
Absolutely. Many production applications integrate several AI services together. For example, a customer support chatbot may use:

- Language   Understanding   (LUIS)   for   intent   recognition

- Azure   OpenAI   for   natural   language   response

- Azure   Cognitive   Search   for   document   retrieval

- Translator   for   multilingual   support

These services are modular and designed to work well together through standard REST APIs and SDKs.

Azure Machine Learning (AML)

Q: Do I need to use Azure ML Studio or can I just use the SDK?

A:
You can use either, depending on your preference and project complexity.

- AML   Studio   provides   a   visual,   code-optional   interface.

- AML SDK (Python) offers full control over training scripts, environments, pipelines, and deployments.
  Most production workflows eventually rely on the SDK or CLI for automation and reproducibility.

Q: What compute targets can I use in Azure ML?

A:

- **Compute Instances** – Dev/test VMs for notebook use
- **Compute Clusters** – Autoscaling clusters for training and inference
- **Inference Clusters** – Managed endpoints on Azure Kubernetes Service
- **Attached VMs or Kubernetes clusters** – Bring your own infrastructure

Each has specific use cases and billing models. Compute Clusters are the most cost-effective for scheduled model training jobs.

Q: Can I deploy ONNX models in Azure ML?

A:
Yes. Azure ML supports ONNX models, which are ideal for cross-platform deployment and optimized inference. You can deploy them using `InferenceConfig` and a scoring script just like Python-based models.

Azure OpenAI

Q: How is Azure OpenAI different from OpenAI.com?

A:
Azure OpenAI provides the same model family (e.g., GPT-4, Codex) but adds:

- Enterprise security and compliance
- Regional data residency
- VNet and private endpoint support
- Managed deployments via Azure Resource Manager It integrates easily with other Azure services, and usage is billed via Azure consumption.

Q: How do I fine-tune a GPT model in Azure OpenAI?

A:
Azure OpenAI now supports fine-tuning for GPT-3.5. Fine-tuning involves:

1. Formatting training data using JSONL

2. Uploading the dataset

3. Starting a fine-tune job via REST API or CLI

4. Using the fine-tuned deployment in inference requests

Fine-tuning GPT-4 is not currently supported but may be in the future.

Q: How do I secure Azure OpenAI endpoints?

A:

- Use Azure AD authentication for enterprise applications

- Enable VNet integration

- Set up role-based access control (RBAC)

- Monitor traffic with Azure Monitor + Network Watcher

- Store secrets in Azure Key Vault and rotate keys regularly

Cognitive Services

Q: Are there usage limits for Cognitive Services APIs?

A:
Yes. Each Cognitive Service has pricing tiers (F0, S0, S1, etc.) with usage caps:

- F0 is free but limited (e.g., 5K text records/month)

- S0+ offers larger quotas and higher performance Check usage in Azure Portal → Cognitive Services → Metrics or Quotas.

Q: Can I deploy Cognitive Services on-prem or to edge devices?

A:
Yes. Microsoft offers **Cognitive Services Containers**, which can be deployed anywhere Docker is supported, including:

- On-prem   servers
- Edge   gateways   (e.g.,   Azure   Stack   Edge)
- IoT   devices   with   compute   capability

Cost and Optimization

Q: How do I estimate the cost of running a model in production?

A:
Use the Azure Pricing Calculator for rough estimates. For ML models:

- Factor in training compute time, VM type (GPU/CPU), data storage, and endpoint availability
- Include   costs   for   logging,   monitoring,   and   networking

Azure Cost Management + Azure Advisor can provide real usage insights and recommendations.

Q: How do I reduce AI inference costs?

A:

- Use batch endpoints for high-volume but low-latency-insensitive workloads
- Deploy   models   with   auto-scale   policies
- Quantize   models   to   reduce   compute   size   (ONNX   +   float16)
- Consider running simpler tasks with Cognitive Services instead of custom ML models
- Monitor   API   call   rates   and   optimize   prompt   length   (for   OpenAI)

Responsible AI

Q: What tools are available for ensuring fairness and transparency?

A:
Azure offers:

- **Responsible AI Dashboard** (visual insights into model behavior)

- **Fairlearn** (bias detection and mitigation)

- **InterpretML** (feature importance, SHAP values)

- **Data Drift Monitor** (detects distribution changes)

You can integrate these into Azure ML pipelines and Jupyter Notebooks.

Q: Can I explain decisions made by a deployed model?

A:
Yes. You can generate local and global explanations using SHAP or LIME. Azure ML supports registering explainers alongside models and returning insights from endpoints.

Example usage:

```
from interpret.ext.blackbox import TabularExplainer
from sklearn.ensemble import RandomForestClassifier

explainer = TabularExplainer(model, X_test)
shap_values = explainer.explain_global()
shap_values.visualize()
```

DevOps and Integration

Q: How can I implement CI/CD for AI models in Azure?

A:
Use:

- **Azure DevOps Pipelines** or **GitHub Actions** for build-test-deploy flows

- Model registration with version control in Azure ML

- Deployment via `mlflow` or `azureml.core`

- Promotion across environments (dev → staging → prod) with approval gates

Q: Can I use Terraform or Bicep to deploy Azure ML infrastructure?

A:
Yes. Azure Machine Learning resources (workspace, compute, endpoints) are fully supported in:

- **Terraform** (via `azurerm_machine_learning_workspace`)

- **Bicep** (ARM templates with simplified syntax)

This enables infrastructure-as-code for reproducible ML environments.

Troubleshooting

Q: My model inference is slow. What should I check?

A:

- Confirm your model is running on appropriate hardware (e.g., GPU if needed)

- Check input preprocessing: avoid inefficient loops or unbatched input

- Review endpoint logs for latency bottlenecks

- Use `azureml-telemetry` to trace model performance

- Consider asynchronous or batch inference for large payloads

Q: I'm getting an HTTP 429 error. What does it mean?

A:
HTTP 429 = Too Many Requests. You've hit your quota. Solutions:

- Throttle request rate

- Upgrade pricing tier

- Contact Microsoft for quota increase

- Use retry/backoff logic in your code

Summary

This FAQ captures real questions asked by Azure AI developers in the field. As Azure's AI capabilities expand, new services, limitations, and best practices emerge—making it essential to revisit documentation, community forums, and changelogs regularly.

This appendix marks the end of your structured journey through the Azure AI landscape. You now have the foundational knowledge, tools, and practical insights to build intelligent, scalable, and responsible AI solutions using Microsoft's cloud ecosystem. Keep building, keep experimenting—and most importantly, keep learning.

www.ingramcontent.com/pod-product-compliance
Lightning Source LLC
La Vergne TN
LVHW022335060326
832902LV00022B/4052